THIS BOOK MAY BE RENEWED

The
Department
of the Treasury

KNOW YOUR GOVERNMENT

The Department of the Treasury

Mark Walston

CHELSEA HOUSE PUBLISHERS

On the cover: Gold bullion at the Federal Reserve Bank in New York City.
Frontis: A high-speed sheet-fed rotary press at the Bureau of Engraving and Printing.

Chelsea House Publishers
Editor-in-Chief: Nancy Toff
Executive Editor: Remmel T. Nunn
Managing Editor: Karyn Gullen Browne
Copy Chief: Juliann Barbato
Picture Editor: Adrian G. Allen
Art Director: Maria Epes
Manufacturing Manager: Gerald Levine

Know Your Government
Senior Editor: Kathy Kuhtz

Staff for THE DEPARTMENT OF THE TREASURY
Copy Editor: Philip Koslow
Deputy Copy Chief: Nicole Bowen
Editorial Assistant: Elizabeth Nix
Picture Researcher: Dixon and Turner Research Associates, Inc.
Picture Coordinator: Michèle Brisson
Assistant Art Director: Loraine Machlin
Senior Designer: Noreen M. Lamb
Production Coordinator: Joseph Romano

First Printing

1 3 5 7 9 8 6 4 2

Library of Congress Cataloging-in-Publication Data
Walston, Mark, 1954–
    The Department of the Treasury/ Mark Walston.
        p.   cm.—(Know your government)
    Bibliography: p.
    1. United States. Dept. of the Treasury.   I. Title.   II. Series:
Know your government (New York, N.Y.)
MJ 261.W36 1989
353.2—dc19

ISBN 0-87754-848-X   89-931
        0-7910-0891-6 (pbk.)   CIP

CONTENTS

KNOW YOUR GOVERNMENT

CHELSEA HOUSE PUBLISHERS

BERKELEY HIGH SCHOOL

100
YEARS
OF
LIBRARY

INTRODUCTION

Government: Crises of Confidence

Arthur M. Schlesinger, jr.

From the start, Americans have regarded their government with a mixture of reliance and mistrust. The men who founded the republic did not doubt the indispensability of government. "If men were angels," observed the 51st Federalist Paper, "no government would be necessary." But men are not angels. Because human beings are subject to wicked as well as to noble impulses, government was deemed essential to assure freedom and order.

At the same time, the American revolutionaries knew that government could also become a source of injury and oppression. The men who gathered in Philadelphia in 1787 to write the Constitution therefore had two purposes in mind. They wanted to establish a strong central authority and to limit that central authority's capacity to abuse its power.

To prevent the abuse of power, the Founding Fathers wrote two basic principles into the new Constitution. The principle of federalism divided power between the state governments and the central authority. The principle of the separation of powers subdivided the central authority itself into three branches—the executive, the legislative, and the judiciary—so that "each may be a check on the other." The *Know Your Government* series focuses on the major executive departments and agencies in these branches of the federal government.

The Constitution did not plan the executive branch in any detail. After vesting the executive power in the president, it assumed the existence of "executive departments" without specifying what these departments should be. Congress began defining their functions in 1789 by creating the Departments of State, Treasury, and War. The secretaries in charge of these departments made up President Washington's first cabinet. Congress also provided for a legal officer, and President Washington soon invited the attorney general, as he was called, to attend cabinet meetings. As need required, Congress created more executive departments.

Setting up the cabinet was only the first step in organizing the American state. With almost no guidance from the Constitution, President Washington, seconded by Alexander Hamilton, his brilliant secretary of the treasury, equipped the infant republic with a working administrative structure. The Federalists believed in both executive energy and executive accountability and set high standards for public appointments. The Jeffersonian opposition had less faith in strong government and preferred local government to the central authority. But when Jefferson himself became president in 1801, although he set out to change the direction of policy, he found no reason to alter the framework the Federalists had erected.

By 1801 there were about 3,000 federal civilian employees in a nation of a little more than 5 million people. Growth in territory and population steadily enlarged national responsibilities. Thirty years later, when Jackson was president, there were more than 11,000 government workers in a nation of 13 million. The federal establishment was increasing at a faster rate than the population.

Jackson's presidency brought significant changes in the federal service. He believed that the executive branch contained too many officials who saw their jobs as "species of property" and as "a means of promoting individual interest." Against the idea of a permanent service based on life tenure, Jackson argued for the periodic redistribution of federal offices, contending that this was the democratic way and that official duties could be made "so plain and simple that men of intelligence may readily qualify themselves for their performance." He called this policy rotation-in-office. His opponents called it the spoils system.

In fact, partisan legend exaggerated the extent of Jackson's removals. More than 80 percent of federal officeholders retained their jobs. Jackson discharged no larger a proportion of government workers than Jefferson had done a generation earlier. But the rise in these years of mass political parties gave federal patronage new importance as a means of building the party and of rewarding activists. Jackson's successors were less restrained in the distribu-

8

tion of spoils. As the federal establishment grew—to nearly 40,000 by 1861—the politicization of the public service excited increasing concern.

After the Civil War the spoils system became a major political issue. High-minded men condemned it as the root of all political evil. The spoilsmen, said the British commentator James Bryce, "have distorted and depraved the mechanism of politics." Patronage, by giving jobs to unqualified, incompetent, and dishonest persons, lowered the standards of public service and nourished corrupt political machines. Office-seekers pursued presidents and cabinet secretaries without mercy. "Patronage," said Ulysses S. Grant after his presidency, "is the bane of the presidential office." "Every time I appoint someone to office," said another political leader, "I make a hundred enemies and one ingrate." George William Curtis, the president of the National Civil Service Reform League, summed up the indictment. He said,

> The theory which perverts public trusts into party spoils, making public
> employment dependent upon personal favor and not on proved merit,
> necessarily ruins the self-respect of public employees, destroys the
> function of party in a republic, prostitutes elections into a desperate
> strife for personal profit, and degrades the national character by lower-
> ing the moral tone and standard of the country.

The object of civil service reform was to promote efficiency and honesty in the public service and to bring about the ethical regeneration of public life. Over bitter opposition from politicians, the reformers in 1883 passed the Pendleton Act, establishing a bipartisan Civil Service Commission, competitive examinations, and appointment on merit. The Pendleton Act also gave the president authority to extend by executive order the number of "classified" jobs—that is, jobs subject to the merit system. The act applied initially only to about 14,000 of the more than 100,000 federal positions. But by the end of the 19th century 40 percent of federal jobs had moved into the classified category.

Civil service reform was in part a response to the growing complexity of American life. As society grew more organized and problems more technical, official duties were no longer so plain and simple that any person of intelligence could perform them. In public service, as in other areas, the all-round man was yielding ground to the expert, the amateur to the professional. The excesses of the spoils system thus provoked the counter-ideal of scientific public administration, separate from politics and, as far as possible, insulated against it.

The cult of the expert, however, had its own excesses. The idea that administration could be divorced from policy was an illusion. And in the realm of policy, the expert, however much segregated from partisan politics, can never attain perfect objectivity. He remains the prisoner of his own set of values. It is these values rather than technical expertise that determine fundamental judgments of public policy. To turn over such judgments to experts, moreover, would be to abandon democracy itself; for in a democracy final decisions must be made by the people and their elected representatives. "The business of the expert," the British political scientist Harold Laski rightly said, "is to be on tap and not on top."

Politics, however, were deeply ingrained in American folkways. This meant intermittent tension between the presidential government, elected every four years by the people, and the permanent government, which saw presidents come and go while it went on forever. Sometimes the permanent government knew better than its political masters; sometimes it opposed or sabotaged valuable new initiatives. In the end a strong president with effective cabinet secretaries could make the permanent government responsive to presidential purpose, but it was often an exasperating struggle.

The struggle within the executive branch was less important, however, than the growing impatience with bureaucracy in society as a whole. The 20th century saw a considerable expansion of the federal establishment. The Great Depression and the New Deal led the national government to take on a variety of new responsibilities. The New Deal extended the federal regulatory apparatus. By 1940, in a nation of 130 million people, the number of federal workers for the first time passed the 1 million mark. The Second World War brought federal civilian employment to 3.8 million in 1945. With peace, the federal establishment declined to around 2 million by 1950. Then growth resumed, reaching 2.8 million by the 1980s.

The New Deal years saw rising criticism of "big government" and "bureaucracy." Businessmen resented federal regulation. Conservatives worried about the impact of paternalistic government on individual self-reliance, on community responsibility, and on economic and personal freedom. The nation in effect renewed the old debate between Hamilton and Jefferson in the early republic, although with an ironic exchange of positions. For the Hamiltonian constituency, the "rich and well-born," once the advocate of affirmative government, now condemned government intervention, while the Jeffersonian constituency, the plain people, once the advocate of a weak central government and of states' rights, now favored government intervention.

In the 1980s, with the presidency of Ronald Reagan, the debate has burst out with unusual intensity. According to conservatives, government intervention abridges liberty, stifles enterprise, and is inefficient, wasteful, and arbitrary. It disturbs the harmony of the self-adjusting market and creates worse troubles than it solves. Get government off our backs, according to the popular cliché, and our problems will solve themselves. When government is necessary, let it be at the local level, close to the people. Above all, stop the inexorable growth of the federal government.

In fact, for all the talk about the "swollen" and "bloated" bureaucracy, the federal establishment has not been growing as inexorably as many Americans seem to believe. In 1949, it consisted of 2.1 million people. Thirty years later, while the country had grown by 70 million, the federal force had grown only by 750,000. Federal workers were a smaller percentage of the population in 1985 than they were in 1955—or in 1940. The federal establishment, in short, has not kept pace with population growth. Moreover, national defense and the postal service account for 60 percent of federal employment.

Why then the widespread idea about the remorseless growth of government? It is partly because in the 1960s the national government assumed new and intrusive functions: affirmative action in civil rights, environmental protection, safety and health in the workplace, community organization, legal aid to the poor. Although this enlargement of the federal regulatory role was accompanied by marked growth in the size of government on all levels, the expansion has taken place primarily in state and local government. Whereas the federal force increased by only 27 percent in the 30 years after 1950, the state and local government force increased by an astonishing 212 percent.

Despite the statistics, the conviction flourishes in some minds that the national government is a steadily growing behemoth swallowing up the liberties of the people. The foes of Washington prefer local government, feeling it is closer to the people and therefore allegedly more responsive to popular needs. Obviously there is a great deal to be said for settling local questions locally. But local government is characteristically the government of the locally powerful. Historically, the way the locally powerless have won their human and constitutional rights has often been through appeal to the national government. The national government has vindicated racial justice against local bigotry, defended the Bill of Rights against local vigilantism, and protected natural resources against local greed. It has civilized industry and secured the rights of labor organizations. Had the states' rights creed prevailed, there would perhaps still be slavery in the United States.

The national authority, far from diminishing the individual, has given most Americans more personal dignity and liberty than ever before. The individual freedoms destroyed by the increase in national authority have been in the main the freedom to deny black Americans their rights as citizens; the freedom to put small children to work in mills and immigrants in sweatshops; the freedom to pay starvation wages, require barbarous working hours, and permit squalid working conditions; the freedom to deceive in the sale of goods and securities; the freedom to pollute the environment—all freedoms that, one supposes, a civilized nation can readily do without.

"Statements are made," said President John F. Kennedy in 1963, "labelling the Federal Government an outsider, an intruder, an adversary. . . . The United States Government is not a stranger or not an enemy. It is the people of fifty states joining in a national effort. . . . Only a great national effort by a great people working together can explore the mysteries of space, harvest the products at the bottom of the ocean, and mobilize the human, natural, and material resources of our lands."

So an old debate continues. However, Americans are of two minds. When pollsters ask large, spacious questions—Do you think government has become too involved in your lives? Do you think government should stop regulating business?—a sizable majority opposes big government. But when asked specific questions about the practical work of government—Do you favor social security? unemployment compensation? Medicare? health and safety standards in factories? environmental protection? government guarantee of jobs for everyone seeking employment? price and wage controls when inflation threatens?—a sizable majority approves of intervention.

In general, Americans do not want less government. What they want is more efficient government. They want government to do a better job. For a time in the 1970s, with Vietnam and Watergate, Americans lost confidence in the national government. In 1964, more than three-quarters of those polled had thought the national government could be trusted to do right most of the time. By 1980 only one-quarter was prepared to offer such trust. But by 1984 trust in the federal government to manage national affairs had climbed back to 45 percent.

Bureaucracy is a term of abuse. But it is impossible to run any large organization, whether public or private, without a bureaucracy's division of labor and hierarchy of authority. And we live in a world of large organizations. Without bureaucracy modern society would collapse. The problem is not to abolish bureaucracy, but to make it flexible, efficient, and capable of innovation.

Two hundred years after the drafting of the Constitution, Americans still regard government with a mixture of reliance and mistrust—a good combination. Mistrust is the best way to keep government reliable. Informed criticism is the means of correcting governmental inefficiency, incompetence, and arbitrariness; that is, of best enabling government to play its essential role. For without government, we cannot attain the goals of the Founding Fathers. Without an understanding of government, we cannot have the informed criticism that makes government do the job right. It is the duty of every American citizen to know our government—which is what this series is all about.

General George Washington reviews the Continental army troops during the Revolution. The Congress had to wrestle with the problem of providing funds to outfit the army and pay soldiers' salaries. It decided to create its own paper money and relied on each state to help pay off the public debt.

ONE

Managing America's Finances

From its founding in 1789, the Department of the Treasury has been one of the federal government's most vital and varied departments. Chief among its concerns has been the management of the nation's finances. From collecting taxes to printing currency, the Treasury, with its 11 bureaus, has played a central role in the development of the United States and its economy.

When the first Congress under the Constitution created the first federal agency—the Customs Service—in 1789 to regulate and collect taxes imposed on imports, it was responding to a primary concern not only of the new government but of the new nation: the need for money. But revenues alone were not enough. The pressing fiscal concerns of the fledgling nation—discharging the huge war debt, establishing public credit (the means of borrowing and lending money), strengthening and stabilizing the federal government—demanded that a central organization be created to manage the country's financial affairs. Accordingly, on September 2, 1789, Congress established the Department of the Treasury, under which the Customs Service and all other financial services would be placed.

The Treasury Department quickly became the dominant organization in the new government, due in large part to the importance of its functions, its size, and its leadership. The latter element came in the beginning from the dynamic personality of Alexander Hamilton, the first secretary of the Treasury, appointed by President George Washington in 1789. Under Hamilton's leadership, and that of successive secretaries into the 19th century, the Treasury Department steadily increased in importance. By 1800, it was the largest of all federal agencies and the one in which the greatest expansion occurred. From the start, a variety of services crucial to the nation's development would reside in the Treasury Department: the collection of the revenue, the management of the public debt, the regulation of the national banking system; the protection of the manufactures of American industry from foreign competition through the regulation of tariffs; and the defense of the country's borders by enforcing customs laws.

By the mid-19th century, the Treasury had taken its place as the federal government's most wide-ranging and influential field organization. Its collectors of customs became the most prominent body of federal agents dealing directly with citizens; to the public economy, they became figures of equal importance. Their diligent collection of the duties, or import taxes, would allow America by the 1830s to rid itself—if ever so briefly—of its lingering national debt. Additionally, the revenues generated by the Treasury Department would pay for the country's westward expansion and would help to build the nation's emerging transportation systems—its canals, its turnpikes, and its railroads.

The responsibilities of the Treasury fluctuated through the years in response to policies established by Congress, the president, and the secretary of the Treasury. Its changing duties also reflected changing national events. During the Civil War, as the Union cast about for the means of financing the lengthy and bloody struggle, the Treasury found itself the testing ground for new programs designed to generate and enhance revenue. Out of the financial experiments during those war years, from 1861 to 1865, came the nation's first income tax; the first national banking system; the Treasury Department's first engraving and printing operation, which issued the first government paper currency; and the beginning of wide-ranging enforcement activities designed to protect the nation's revenues.

At the beginning of the 20th century, as the United States emerged as a world power, expanding its borders and becoming a major force in the international market, the Treasury Department followed along, expanding its own horizons. The explosion of people and products streaming through American ports brought with it increased responsibilities for the Customs Service. As new towns rose in the West, citizens looked to the federal government and the Treasury Department to release more money into the economy and provide the capital needed to build towns, start businesses, and

16

The Government House in New York in 1797. Although originally designed as the presidential residence when New York was the nation's capital, the building later became the governor's mansion and in 1799 New York's first customs house. In July 1789, Congress created the Customs Service as the first federal agency to regulate and collect taxes levied on imported goods.

fund the American dream. Congress and the Treasury responded by restructuring the tax system, by strengthening the nationwide network of national banks, and by creating the means of eliminating money shortages.

When the United States entered World War I in 1917, the burden of managing the nation's wartime finances fell upon the Treasury. The department reacted by stepping up its revenue collection, developing innovative financing programs, and creating new and more efficient agencies to handle the burgeoning public debt. When the United States was drawn into World War II 34 years later, with the Japanese bombing of the Pearl Harbor naval base in Hawaii, the Treasury Department rose once again to the challenge of securing and managing the staggering sums necessary to finance the American war effort.

The Department of the Treasury building on Pennsylvania Avenue in northwest Washington, D.C. Today only about 10 percent of the Treasury's 120,000 employees work here.

As the 20th century progressed, the Treasury Department continued testing a variety of new national programs. In 1919, with the ratification of the Eighteenth Amendment to the Constitution, which prohibited the manufacture, sale, or transport of liquor, it was the Treasury Department that Congress called upon to battle illegal rumrunners (people who engage in bringing prohibited liquor ashore or across a border) and bootleggers (people who produce or distribute liquor illegally). When the Great Depression ravaged the country's economy in the 1930s, it was the Treasury Department that played the key role in implementing the myriad programs intended to restore stability and financial security. And in the 1960s, when the drug problem grew to epidemic proportions, it was the Treasury Department that became the first line of defense in efforts to halt the flow of drugs across U.S. borders.

The variety of responsibilities assigned to the Treasury through the years is reflected today in the diversity of the 11 bureaus operating within the department: the Bureau of Alcohol, Tobacco and Firearms; the Office of the Comptroller of the Currency; the United States Customs Service; the Bureau of Engraving and Printing; the Federal Law Enforcement Training Center; the

18

Financial Management Service; the Internal Revenue Service; the United States Mint; the Bureau of Public Debt; the United States Savings Bonds Division; and the United States Secret Service. Tying the components of the department together, from the secretary of the Treasury on down, is the management of the nation's finances. Through nearly two centuries of collecting taxes, enforcing revenue laws, printing currency, minting coins, managing banks, keeping accounts, and paying off debts, the Department of the Treasury has steered the nation's economy through war, depression, and prosperity.

Members of the Second Continental Congress leave Carpenter's Hall in Phila-delphia after a session. Engrossed in preparing for war with Britain and in finding ways to finance it, the Congress approved the printing of $2 million in paper money.

TWO

The Birth of the Treasury Department

America in the years after the Revolution was a nation in transition. Peace with Britain did not automatically bring accord to the 13 former colonies. The constitution that united them—the Articles of Confederation, adopted by the states in 1781 to form a central government—was, in nature and intent, a compromise among proponents of a strong central government, jealous guardians of states' rights, and a fiercely independent citizenry. The Congress, wrestling constantly with the disparate states to assume the power to govern, was forced to step lightly. Squarely at the center of the debate over how to govern was one overriding concern: money.

Since the country's beginnings, each American Congress has had to contend with the question of how best to fund the nation. For the Second Continental Congress, which met in Philadelphia in the summer of 1775, the need for national finances was of the utmost urgency. Now on an irreversible course toward war with Britain, the Congress called for the raising of six companies of riflemen and appointed George Washington as head of the newly organized Continental army. The government was faced with the perplexing problem of how to provide the funds necessary to outfit the army, pay soldiers' salaries, and carry on the fight.

The American colonies issued "New York dollars," "Pennsylvania shillings," and later "Continental dollars" to bring gold and silver coins into the national treasury during the 1770s. By 1780, however, the value of the Continental currency had fallen to 40 Continental dollars for 1 dollar in silver, giving rise to the expression "not worth a continental."

Yet this Congress had neither the power to levy and collect taxes from its own constituents, nor any tangible basis on which to seek credit (loans) from foreign nations or bankers. The Continental Congress chose the convenient but precarious course of creating its own paper money in the form of bills of credit, or promises to pay, and basing their future redemption in hard money—silver and gold coins—only on the faith of the patriots. The Congress approved the printing of $2 million in bills of credit and appointed a committee of delegates, composed of three prominent businessmen from Pennsylvania—Richard Bache, Stephen Pascall, and Michael Hillegas—to oversee the printing. The committee hired 28 Philadelphians to sign and number each of the bills rolling off the presses.

Ultimately, the Continental Congress looked to the colonies to bring into the national treasury the hard currency required to back up the bills of credit, with each colony bearing an equal share of the weight of the public debt. Gold and silver coins, however, were in short supply in America during the 1770s. With a national mint yet to be established, the coins in circulation were primarily foreign in origin. Spanish dollars, French crowns, and Dutch ducats were all accepted in payment, along with British shillings, pence, and pounds. Some colonies—Massachusetts, for example—began minting their own coins, as did a few enterprising private individuals. Still, hard currency was scarce. Nevertheless, in July 1775 the Congress directed the provincial assemblies to select "a treasurer for their respective colonies" and to provide ways and means to pay in cash their proportion of the bills issued by Congress, "in such manner as may be most effectual and best adapted to the condition, circumstances, and usual mode of levying taxes in such colony." To manage the forthcoming funds, the Congress appointed Michael Hillegas and George Clymer, a Philadelphia merchant, "joint treasurers of the United Colonies," Hillegas to receive the funds, Clymer to pay them out. Each man was required to reside in Philadelphia and to post a bond of $100,000 as "surety for the faithful performance of their office."

In 1775, the Congress appointed Michael Hillegas (left), a prominent businessman from Pennsylvania, and George Clymer (right), a Philadelphia merchant, to be joint treasurers of the united colonies. Hillegas received the revenues coming in to the Treasury from the taxes each colony levied on its citizens, and Clymer paid out the funds to purchase rifles, ammunition, food, and clothing.

Most of the colonists, fired with the desire for independence and sure of the justice of their cause, initially accepted the financial scheme. Many, however, regarded the bills with suspicion; some even refused to consider them as payment for services. To impress upon the people the importance of its plan, Congress went so far as to resolve that if any person "be so lost to all virtue and regard for his country" as to reject the notes, he should be "deemed an enemy of his country."

With each new million in Continental dollars rolling off the presses, providing funds to build warships, buy rifles and ammunition, and feed and clothe the armed forces, the Congress redefined its treasury operations. To keep up with the growing complexity of financing the struggle, the Congress would expand its treasury committee members from 3, to 5, to 13 delegates and eventually devote each Tuesday, Thursday, and Saturday to treasury matters. Yet the constant bickering of the colonies in the Congress and their continuing fear of centralized authority forestalled the creation of an effective and independent treasury. For years the vital functions of the treasury would be managed by a changing parade of congressional committees. Committees accountable only to the Congress, however, did not satisfy the needs of the various colonies who were called upon to make good the paper money of the Congress. Consequently, in April 1776 the Congress established a separate Treasury Office of Accounts, consisting of an auditor general and a corps of clerks, all under the supervision of the Treasury Committee. It was to ensure that "the public records should be regularly stated and kept and justly liquidated and settled." Colonial assemblies and military officers now submitted their accounts to the Treasury Office for settlement.

The work of the Treasury Office was considerably expanded following the Declaration of Independence on July 4, 1776. Now endowed with national status, the Congress sought to fill its treasury war chest by borrowing money from both domestic and foreign sources. Immediately it called for $500,000 in hard currency to be raised "for the use of the United States." Loan offices were established in each state and commissioners were appointed to manage them. These individual state commissioners received the monies from investors and in return issued government securities, that is, notes that promised to pay the borrowed money back with interest. The commissioners also reported and paid the receipts to the main treasury in Philadelphia. Still, all that the Congress offered as collateral (valuable property pledged by a borrower to protect the interests of the lender) for the loans was the good faith of the new nation.

The Congress explored nearly every means of raising money to keep the

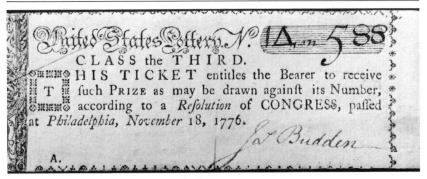

A ticket from the national lottery held in 1776. The Congress supported the Treasury Committee's plan to raise more than $1 million for the support of the American Revolution by holding a national lottery.

drive toward independence going. On November 1, 1776, the Treasury Committee announced a grand plan to raise $1,005,000 for the support of the Continental army by holding a huge national lottery; more than 100,000 tickets would be sold, with prizes ranging from $20 to $50,000. Winning tickets of more than $50 would be paid in treasury notes, redeemable after 5 years. Books of tickets were sent to the various state governors, with the request that the states make wholesale purchases, but the states did not receive the plan enthusiastically. Ticket sales to the public were brisk at first but soon fell off sharply because of the public's declining interest in the scheme. Although the national lottery provided a temporary flow of funds for the Congress to draw on, by the time of the fourth and final lottery drawing, held in 1779, the total amount of money brought in from ticket sales was substantially less than the more than $1 million hoped for by the Congress.

Despite the various attempts to raise money—through printing bills, borrowing, and holding national lotteries—the nation's finances remained in a precarious position. Many of the states, on whom the Congress relied to back its financial schemes, were reluctant to increase the taxes on their own citizens for the sake of the national treasury; many feared they were already carrying a greater share of the financial burden than that of neighboring states. Fighting a war has never been an inexpensive proposition, and so a flood of paper money continued to gush from the government presses; between 1775 and 1779, more than $241 million had been issued. The Congress continued to redefine the Treasury Office, experimenting with different arrangements for handling the accounts. It reorganized the office in 1778 and created a new system: An auditor and accountants examined and approved all claims against the govern-

25

ment, a comptroller verified those accounts and vouchers payable to or by the United States by affixing an official treasury seal, and a treasurer received, stored, and paid out all monies. The following year the Congress tried placing the entire operation under an Office of the Secretary of the Treasury. Finding one person in the United States qualified for such an important position, however, proved difficult. So the Congress sent a communication to England, of all places, to invite Richard Price, a noted British philosopher of economics, to venture across the Atlantic Ocean and direct American finances. Price declined, and the secretary's office, along with that of the comptroller, was abolished later that year when a new Board of Treasury supplanted the older Committee of the Treasury.

But the Congress's inexperience in dealing with finances on a national level and its constricting reliance on the states for funding continued to keep the treasury system weak and ineffectual. No help was to be found in the Articles of Confederation, the new arrangement under which the government operated, ratified by the states in 1781. The Articles specifically denied Congress one important power: the power to tax. Colonial experience had shown that the power to tax could easily become a tool of oppression. In the 1760s, King George III and the British Parliament, trying to establish more efficient rule in the colonies, had laid duties on imports into the colonies, duties that were to be used to pay the salaries of royal governors and judges. The colonists, who were not allowed to elect members of Parliament, later rebelled against the oppressive government and declared their independence from England in 1776. Consequently, Congress, under the Articles of Confederation, was not even allowed to tax imports, for fear that those customs duties would someday jeopardize the liberties of the states. Meanwhile, the Continental currency issued by Congress was steadily declining in value. By 1780 its worth in hard cash had fallen to 40 Continental dollars for $1 in silver. Undaunted, Congress issued an additional $191 million in paper money in January 1781. Within 6 months, however, this currency's value had fallen to $100 of paper money to $1 in silver. Soon the expression "not worth a continental" came into widespread use, in reference to the plummeting value of Congress's paper money.

By the spring of 1781, the national treasury was in a distressing state and the American economy was near total collapse. To pull the new nation out of its slump, Congress turned to Robert Morris, a prominent Philadelphia banker and merchant, appointing him superintendent of finance. Through extensive reorganizational efforts, the securing of loans from the Netherlands and France, and advances from his own pocket, Morris managed to check the crisis before

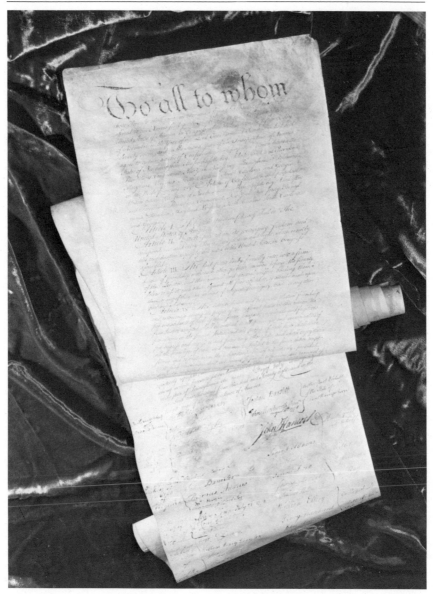

The Articles of Confederation, the precursor of the Constitution, was ratified by the states in 1781 and established the first national government. Under the Articles, Congress could raise money only by asking the states for it; Congress had no power to force a state to pay its share of the government's financial support.

In 1781, Congress appointed Robert Morris, a prominent Philadelphia banker, as superintendent of finance to help pull the country out of its economic crisis. Morris obtained loans from France and the Netherlands, advanced the country money from his own pocket, and reorganized treasury operations.

the year's end. He even secured sufficient funds for General Washington to move his army from New York to Yorktown and eventually force the surrender of the British forces under General Charles Cornwallis.

Morris's tenure as superintendent of finance, was tainted, however, by accusations of irregularities in his accounts and personal speculation (assuming a business risk in the hope of gain, with public funds). To add to the superintendent's problems, in June 1783, following the proclamation of the end of the war with Britain, dissatisfied Continental army veterans marched upon Congress, demanding to be paid the back salaries long owed them by the treasury. The veterans' growing protest forced Congress to temporarily move from Philadelphia to the less threatening confines of Princeton, New Jersey. Despite these troubles, Congress formally acknowledged its debt to Robert Morris, declaring that he conducted the business of the treasury "with great ability and assiduity, in a manner highly advantageous to the United States, and in conformity with the system laid down by Congress." Since his appointment, Congress declared, the public accounts "have been regularly and punctually kept, . . . many of the accounts which preceded this institution have already been settled, and most of the others put into a train of adjustment." Morris would continue to serve as superintendent of finance until 1784, when ill health forced him to retire. Thereafter, Congress placed the treasury operations under a three-member Board of Treasury.

Although the end of the revolutionary war in 1783 brought peace and independence to the land, it seemed only to magnify the nation's financial troubles. By 1786, the shortage of hard currency and the persistent clamor of creditors brought the postwar depression (a period of low economic activity marked by rising levels of unemployment) to an all-time low. State taxes climbed higher and higher to pay off the war debt. Under the Articles of Confederation each state was permitted to set its own tariffs and collect its own duties, allowing states to place exorbitant rates not only upon foreign imports but on the products of the other states. New York required poultry dealers from New Jersey to line up at the border, have their eggs counted and their hens weighed, and pay duties before doing business. Firewood from Connecticut was measured and counted before it could be sold in New York; Connecticut merchants alone paid more than 40,000 British pounds annually in New York customs duties, little of which ever made its way into the national treasury. The economic crisis threatened to tear apart the bonds of the infant nation. As Noah Webster, the noted author of dictionaries, commented in 1785, "Our pretended union is but a name, and our confederation a cobweb."

At the root of the problems was a weak Congress that lacked the authority

The surrender of the British troops led by General Cornwallis (standing, center) at Yorktown on October 19, 1781. Superintendent of Finance Morris managed to raise the money that enabled General Washington (on white horse) to move his army to Yorktown.

to raise its own operating funds, relying entirely upon the generosity of the states for its survival. Members of the Congress realized that no national government could survive upon the paltry allowance paid by the states. A new federal government was needed, one that could enforce the collection of taxes and force the states to pay their share. The young nation would then be able to pull itself out of its staggering debt.

Ultimately, the U.S. Constitution provided for a new central government. Its framers, meeting in convention in Philadelphia during the torrid summer of

1787, knew by experience the difficulties of trying to raise an army, fight a war, and run a government on borrowed funds. The new government that they were creating would not be forced to operate under the same debilitating conditions; it would have power under the Constitution "to lay and collect taxes, duties, imposts and excises," provided that they fell on each state with equal weight. And by ratifying the Constitution during 1788, the states voluntarily transferred to the new federal government their right to collect and retain customs duties.

Under the Constitution it was the responsibility of the newly created House of Representatives to originate all revenue bills. Immediately after the swearing-in of the first House of Representatives at Federal Hall in New York City on April 8, 1789, Representative James Madison of Virginia rose from his seat to introduce a subject he declared to be "of the greatest magnitude," a subject that required Congress's "first attention and united exertions."

Howard Chandler Christy's 1940 painting Scene at the Signing of the Constitution of the United States. *When the states ratified the Constitution during 1788, they transferred to the new federal government their right to collect and keep customs duties. Congress was given the power to establish and collect taxes, borrow and coin money, and appropriate money for government operations.*

31

"The deficiency in our treasury," Madison noted, "is too notorious to make it necessary" to comment upon. Instead, Madison continued, "let us content ourselves with endeavoring to remedy the evil. To do this, a national revenue must be obtained. But the system must be a one that, while it secures the object of revenue, it shall not be oppressive to our constituents. Happy it is for us that such a system is within our power; for I apprehend that both these objects may be obtained from an impost on articles imported into the United States."

By May 16, the House, acting upon Madison's proposal, had passed and sent on to the Senate its first significant piece of legislation, a bill "for levying a duty on goods, wares, and merchandises imported into the United States." This first Tariff Act, signed into law by President Washington on July 4, 1789, was considered so important that the press of the day hailed it as a "second Declaration of Independence." As Representative Fisher Ames of Massachusetts expressed it: "Revenue is the soul of government, and if such a soul had not been breathed into our body politic it would have been a lifeless carcass, fit only to be buried."

With the means of generating revenue thus firmly established, the House then took up the issue of creating an executive department to handle the country's future revenues, funded by import duties levied under the Tariff Act. Representative Elias Boudinot of New Jersey expressed the urgent need for such a department. "Our national debt is considerable," he exclaimed to the House on May 19, "and it will be attended with the most dreadful consequences to let these affairs run into confusion and ruin for want of proper regulations to keep them in order." Boudinot rejected the former treasury offices as appropriate models, "by reason of the essential change which has taken place in government" under the Constitution. Instead, Boudinot proposed that the House establish an entirely new office "for the management of the finances of the United States, at the head of which shall be an officer to be denominated the Secretary of Finance." Representative Egbert Benson of New York wholeheartedly approved of the new executive department. But in place of "Finance," Benson suggested the new office be termed "the Treasury Department."

Creating the Treasury Department, however, proved to be a thorny proposition. Quickly, the debates in Congress centered around a crucial point: Should the powers of the Treasury be vested in a single individual or in a board of commissioners? Elbridge Gerry of Massachusetts, a former Treasury commissioner in the Continental Congress, expressed his fear of placing too much control in the hands of one individual. "By such an arrangement," Gerry argued, "we put his integrity to the trial. If he is disposed to embezzle the public money, it will be out of the power of the Executive itself to check or control him in his nefarious practices." Instead, Gerry proposed that power to direct the Treasury be safely diffused in a board of three commissioners, one taken from each "grand division of the United States, namely the Eastern, the Middle, and Southern Districts."

Congressman Abraham Baldwin of Georgia, however, was convinced that there was "not so much responsibility in boards as there was in individuals. . . . Boards were generally more destitute of energy than was an individual placed at the head of a Department." And yet he did not advocate unlimited authority. Baldwin hoped to see proper checks provided in the form of a comptroller (one who supervises expenditures), auditors (those who examine and verify accounts), a register (keeper of records), and a treasurer (one who receives, stores, and disburses revenues). The secretary should not be allowed "to touch a farthing of the public money beyond his salary. The settling of accounts should be in the Auditors and Comptroller, the registering to be in another officer, and the cash in the hands of one unconnected with either. In this way, the Treasury might be safe, and great improvements made in the business of the revenue."

James Madison endorsed this arrangement. With such a separation of duties, he reasoned, not only would adequate controls be put in place, but the secretary of the Treasury would be able "to employ his time and talents in rendering essential services to his country." Guided by the general outline, the House hammered out the details of a bill establishing "a Department of the Treasury, in which shall be the following officers, namely: a Secretary of the Treasury, to be deemed head of the Department; a Comptroller, an Auditor, a Treasurer, a Register, and an Assistant to the Secretary, which Assistant shall be appointed by said Secretary." As head of the department, the secretary would be responsible for preparing plans for the management of the revenue and support of the public credit; for preparing estimates of yearly revenues and expenditures; for supervising the collection of the revenue; for overseeing the sale of public lands; for deciding on forms of keeping and stating accounts; and for responding to Congress on all matters relative to finances. The day-to-day operations of the Treasury would be in the hands of the auditor, comptroller, treasurer, and register, who collectively would receive the public accounts, certify the balances, and keep a record of all the accounts of receipts and expenditures of the public money and of all debts due to or from the United States. The treasurer would be responsible for receiving and keeping all the monies of the United States and disbursing them upon warrants

Alexander Hamilton, appointed secretary of the Treasury by President Washington in 1789, proposed that the entire $50 million of the public debt be funded at face value rather than at its reduced market value. He also proposed that the federal government assume the states' debts, thus binding public creditors to the national interest rather than to the individual states.

(purchase orders) drawn by the secretary, countersigned by the comptroller, and recorded by the register.

Each of these Treasury officers would be bound by the concluding section of the bill, proposed by Representative Adenaus Burke of South Carolina, which prohibited any of the persons appointed from being "directly or indirectly concerned in commerce, or in speculating the public funds, under a high penalty, and being deemed guilty of a high crime or misdemeanor."

On September 2, 1789, President Washington signed into law the bill creating the Department of the Treasury. To the post of secretary Washington appointed his former aide-de-camp, the brilliant 34-year-old lawyer from New York, Alexander Hamilton. Only 10 days after Hamilton took office, the House of Representatives, anxious to set the nation's finances on their proper course, called upon the secretary to prepare and report a comprehensive plan for the "adequate support of the public credit." That report to Congress, the first section of which was delivered in January 1790, demonstrated Hamilton's firm grasp of the importance of sound fiscal underpinnings in the development of the new nation. "The debt of the United States," Hamilton wrote, "was the price of liberty. The faith of America was pledged for it, and with solemnities that give peculiar force to the obligation." Now the time had come, Hamilton urged, to make good those promises, and in his report he set forth the principles by which Congress and the Treasury should proceed. Foremost, as a full return of the faith of those who invested in the War of Independence, Hamilton proposed that the entire $50 million national debt be funded at face value rather than its depreciated, or reduced, market value. This would be done by calling in the old certificates of indebtedness and exchanging them for new securities, some earning 6 percent interest, some 3 percent, and others with the interest on the remainder deferred for 10 years. In other words, one debt would be paid off by creating another.

Next, Hamilton proposed that the federal government assume the debts of the various states, adding more than $20 million to the total debt to be carried by the Department of the Treasury. If the Treasury assumed the state debts, Hamilton argued, and paid them off at face value, public creditors (those to whom money is owed) would be bound to the national interest rather than that of the individual states. Hamilton advocated the establishment of a Bank of the United States to assist the Treasury in discharging its obligations. The bank would be modeled after the Bank of England: It would assist the federal government by acting as a repository for the collected taxes, disbursing government salaries, controlling the issue of paper money, and generally aiding in servicing the debt. Hard currency from customs duties would back this

The Bank of the United States in Philadelphia in 1799. Secretary Hamilton proposed the creation of the First Bank, and, despite congressional opposition, in 1791 President Washington signed the bill giving the Bank a 20-year charter.

program. Additional revenues would accrue from the sale of public lands in the West and various internal taxes enacted from time to time.

Not all of Hamilton's proposals found unanimous favor. Many in Congress felt that allowing the exchange of old securities—both state and national—at face value was an injustice to those who were forced to sell their paper securities well below face value just to get the cash necessary to keep families and businesses going. They also believed that the plan favored the wealthy merchants and speculators of the northern seaports who had bought up those depreciated securities from the common people and would be able to profit by redeeming them. Eventually, after some political bargaining, Hamilton's funding and assumption proposals (those measures used by the federal government to take over the debts incurred by the states during the American Revolution) passed Congress and became law on August 4, 1790.

As for Hamilton's plan for a Bank of the United States, some regarded it as unconstitutional. Foremost among the opponents was Thomas Jefferson, Washington's secretary of state. To Jefferson's mind, such a bank, although perhaps convenient to Hamilton's plan, could not be regarded as essential, and consequently did not come under the constitutional power granted to Congress "to make all laws necessary and proper" for executing its programs. Jefferson argued that existing banks, such as the state bank in Philadelphia, could just as easily handle the Treasury funds.

Hamilton, on the other hand, adopted a looser interpretation of the Constitution. "If the end be clearly comprehended within any of the specified powers," Hamilton reasoned, "and if the measure have an obvious relation to that end, and is not forbidden by any particular provision of the Constitution, it may safely be deemed to come within the compass of the national authority." Hamilton was quick to point out that Congress had already acted upon that theory by authorizing the Treasury Department to build and maintain a series of lighthouses along the Atlantic shore, as "necessary to the proper regulation of commerce." Such aids to navigation had already been established by the states; the act of 1789 had actually called for the transfer to federal ownership of lighthouses previously constructed by the states. The proposed Bank of the United States merely followed precedents set by Congress. President Washington, weighing both opinions, eventually sided with his secretary of the Treasury, and on February 25, 1791, he signed the Bank bill, chartering its operation for 20 years.

Under Hamilton's dynamic leadership, the Treasury Department quickly became the dominant organization in the new government. He took full advantage of the fact that nearly every phase of public policy involved finance and did not hesitate to throw himself into foreign and military as well as domestic affairs. Hamilton soon became a fixture in the chambers of Congress; as Senator William Maclay of Pennsylvania noted, "Nothing is done [in the House of Representatives] without him." Hamilton would arrive early in the morning to wait on the Speaker of the House and would spend the rest of the day "running from place to place among the members," offering his advice and opinion on upcoming bills. As a result, many diverse functions fell under the Treasury Department's control. In addition to regulating the collection of customs duties, the Treasury Department would assume responsibility for

The Massachusetts, *the first and largest of the original 10 revenue cutters used by the Treasury Department to patrol American waters and enforce revenue laws.*

building and maintaining a fleet of revenue cutters, or armed sailing ships used for patrolling American waters, and enforcing the revenue laws. It would also take charge of constructing lighthouses and other navigational aids, conducting land surveys of the United States, providing medical care for seamen, and paying veterans' pensions. The Treasury would oversee establishing the nation's standards for weights and measures and, until the Post Office Department was established in 1792, running the mails. By 1800, the Treasury

Department had nearly 1,700 employees, more than half of the total federal civil service.

Not all of the Treasury's programs were regarded by the American people as necessary to the nation's finances. To augment the revenues generated by customs duties, Hamilton prevailed upon Congress to set up a system of internal taxes and an organization to collect them. Excise taxes (taxes levied on the manufacture, transportation, sale, or consumption of goods) were placed upon spirits (liquor), sugar, snuff, bonds, and slaves, and a federal property tax was placed on houses. Some 400 revenue officers were appointed to collect the taxes. Their efforts, however, proved unpopular to Americans still hostile to taxation, who remembered that it was the oppressive tax policies of Great Britain that gave rise to their rebellion. In 1791, the Treasury's tax assessor in Savannah, Georgia, complained to Hamilton about "the great disfavor with which these excises are met" and asked how the secretary proposed going about collecting the taxes in the face of mounting resistance. Soon farmers throughout the southern and mid-Atlantic states protested the tax on spirits; they regularly disposed of surplus grain by distilling it into whiskey and did not want to be assessed for this manufacture. Opposition to the tax eventually escalated into armed confrontation in Pennsylvania, where federal troops had to be called out to quash a group of rifle-bearing farmers in the so-called Whiskey Rebellion of 1794. Internal taxes, however, never really added significantly to the early federal revenues; by 1800, customs duties were bringing in more than $5 million in receipts, compared to $400,000 in internal revenues. In 1802, Thomas Jefferson, newly elected president, would persuade Congress to abolish all internal taxes, leaving customs duties as the greatest source of Treasury revenues. (Other revenues included monies received in federal land sales.)

Perhaps even more unsettling to some Americans was the suspicion that Hamilton's Treasury programs were not always inspired by a simple concern for federal finances. To many, the main beneficiary of his funding and assumption measures appeared to be a select group of wealthy merchants, professional men, and landowners from the northern states who were reaping huge profits from speculating in government securities. Among that group was William Duer, a New York wartime profiteer, a client of Hamilton's in his private law practice, and later his assistant secretary of the Treasury. While in office, Duer had concocted an elaborate scheme involving trading in the depreciated public securities, the success of which depended wholly on his inside knowledge of Hamilton's impending reports to Congress. When Duer's scheme failed and he went bankrupt in the spring of 1792 and "the prince of the

Weapon-bearing farmers tar and feather a Customs Service agent and set fire to his home during the so-called Whiskey Rebellion of 1794. The excise taxes that the Treasury levied on liquor were very unpopular, and the revenue officers responsible for collecting the taxes were often met with open hostility by opposing farmers who disposed of surplus grain by distilling it into whiskey.

tribe of speculators," as he was dubbed, was sentenced to debtor's prison, the scandal fell heavily on Hamilton. By January 1793, repeated charges of corruption and mismanagement leveled against Hamilton culminated in a set of congressional resolutions calling for an official inquiry into the condition of the Treasury Department. Hamilton was never formally charged, but the rumors and allegations severely diminished his standing in the administration. Ultimately, Hamilton's controversial funding programs would drive politicians—and the nation—into opposing camps. The divisiveness in Congress became so intense that in February 1793, Oliver Wolcott, Hamilton's auditor of the Treasury (and two years later his successor as secretary), feared that the funding and assumption policies would eventually tear the nation apart. If they did, he remarked, then perhaps, for the good of the individual states, "the separation ought to be eternal."

Adding to the political fury was the simmering antagonism between Hamilton and Jefferson. At issue were the two men's visions of what this new

A bustling street in New York in 1799 (top). Monticello, Thomas Jefferson's idyllic home in Virginia, circa 1800 (bottom). Hamilton and Jefferson had different visions of what the new nation should be: Hamilton saw the country flourishing because of the growth in manufacturing and commerce and the support of a strong central government dominated by the nation's elite; Jefferson, in contrast, saw America as a country built by the hard work of farmers and supported by a government that stressed the rights of individuals.

41

A 1922 photograph of the first U.S. Mint building in Philadelphia. Congress passed the Mint Act in 1792 to produce much-needed gold, silver, and copper coins. Jefferson managed to exert sufficient political pressure on Congress to have the mint placed under his control in the Department of State.

government and new nation should be. Hamilton saw the future America as a country of diversified industries, dominated by manufacturing and commerce and governed by a strong central government of the nation's elite—the well-educated, wealthy property owners. Jefferson, on the other hand, envisioned America as an agrarian society, one built on farming, democratic in nature, emphasizing rights of individuals as opposed to a strong central government.

By 1791, Jefferson was convinced that Hamilton and his "corrupt squadron" menaced the country with their dreams of an industrial future fueled by the Treasury's funding schemes. Jefferson began to exert political pressure on the Treasury Department, pushing his own nominees for every new opening, while at the same time trying to curtail the department's expansion. In 1792, Congress passed the Mint Act, establishing the nation's first mint in Philadelphia to produce the much-needed gold, silver, and copper coins. The operation, logically an enterprise to come under the authority of the Treasury Department, was instead placed under the supervision of Secretary of State Jefferson.

The unrelenting attacks on Hamilton's policies finally led him to resign his post as secretary of the Treasury in 1794. But before he left, his vigorous leadership and close attention to day-to-day details had transformed the Treasury into the strongest and most comprehensive of all the departments of the young federal government.

A view of the new capital city of Washington, looking down Pennsylvania Avenue, in 1800. The Treasury building was erected next to the president's residence (the building with columns, to the right of the avenue), its location affirming the department's significance in the operations of the government.

THREE

The Years of Growth, 1800–72

In 1800, after 11 years of occupying temporary quarters, first in New York City and then in Philadelphia, the federal government finally arrived at its permanent home on the banks of the Potomac River, on a 10-square-mile district carved out of the states of Maryland and Virginia. Congress christened the new nation's capital "Washington" in honor of the late first president. All of the federal branches took up residence in the new seat of government: Congress in the still-unfinished Capitol building; President John Adams in the Executive Mansion, later to be called the White House. Awaiting the arrival of Secretary of the Treasury Oliver Wolcott, Jr., and his staff was a new Treasury building, standing directly across from the president's house, its location testifying to the department's importance in the scheme of government. Soon the rooms of the small wooden structure, designed by the English architect George Hatfield, were filled with the 69 employees of the main Treasury office, all under the direction of the secretary.

The basic elements that would characterize the Treasury throughout the first half of the 19th century were in place by the time of its arrival in Washington in 1800. At the center of the system was the Customs Service, upon whose shoulders rested the responsibility of bringing in the money that enabled all other branches of the federal government to operate. The main function of the Customs Service was to collect the taxes due on imports coming into American ports. And indeed, until the 1860s the duties collected by the service provided the Treasury with its major source of income. During the service's initial year of operation, 1789–90, customs agents collected more than $2 million. In the ensuing years customs revenues would climb steadily; by the 1830s, they averaged nearly $20 million annually, helping to eliminate the national debt in 1836—for the first and only time in United States history.

Because of its importance to the functioning of the government, the Customs Service quickly became the Treasury's main field agency. Through the 1800s, the majority of the department's employees were assigned to the Customs Service. Customs officers were stationed in every major port along the Atlantic shore, along the Canadian border, and later, after the purchase of the Louisiana Territory from France in 1803 and the annexation of Spanish Florida in the 1820s, all along the Gulf of Mexico. In many of the smaller border and port towns, customs officers were often the only representatives of the federal government; as such, they would be called upon time and again by Congress to perform a number of other tasks in addition to their main function of collecting duties. Many of these tasks, such as the construction of lighthouses and the administration of federal hospitals, would later be taken over by other government agencies.

Although the revenue collections of the Customs Service brought money into the Treasury, it was the U.S. Mint that turned out the hard currency used in America's daily cash transactions. Congress first established the mint under the control of the State Department but made it an independent agency in 1799, accountable directly to the president. From its facility in Philadelphia the mint turned out the hard specie—gold, silver, and copper coins—on which the nation's monetary system depended. Each denomination, or value, of coin was based on the decimal system, first proposed in Congress by Thomas Jefferson in 1785. The American dollar issued by the U.S. Mint was roughly equivalent to the Spanish dollar then still in widespread use in the United States; the smaller coins were fractions of the dollar. The gold, silver, and copper stamped into coins came to the federal mint from a variety of sources: Some was purchased by the federal government in exchange for Treasury securities, some came simply from foreign coins melted down and restamped.

In its first 10 years of production, from 1794 to 1805, the U.S. Mint issued nearly 1½ million silver dollars. Individuals bought up many of these dollars because of their quality and strength of value on the foreign exchange market, for the purpose of exportation, especially to Mexico and the West Indies, where a higher price could be received. As a result, very few of the silver

The Liberty silver dollar issued by the U.S. Mint in 1794. From the Philadelphia mint, the Treasury produced the hard specie, or gold, silver, and copper coins, on which America's monetary system depended.

dollars were left in circulation in the United States. In 1806, Secretary of State James Madison discussed the problem in a letter addressed to the director of the mint, Robert Patterson. "As it is probable further purchases and exportations [of silver dollars] will be made," Madison wrote, "the President directs that all silver to be coined at the mint shall be small denominations, so that the largest piece shall not exceed half a dollar." Consequently, the mint's production of silver dollars was discontinued until 1836, when a small run of 1,000 was issued. Not until three years later, however, would the mint resume its coining of silver dollars on a regular basis.

Under the conditions of the Mint Act of 1792, the U.S. Mint was also charged with coining silver half-dollars, quarter-dollars, dimes, and half-dimes, in addition to the silver dollars. The mint also turned out $10 gold coins, called "eagles" because of the national bird featured prominently on the face, along with gold half-eagles ($5) and quarter-eagles ($2.50). Copper cents and half-cents rounded out the coins produced by the U.S. Mint.

Managing the revenues brought in by the Customs Service and paying out the money required to sustain the various federal departments and programs was a Treasury system relatively unchanged from that established by the original act. That act provided for a system of receiving, safeguarding, and disbursing public funds. In addition, Congress directed the secretary of the Treasury to maintain an accounting system that would keep track of the federal government's receipts and expenditures. Initially, Congress gave the treasurer of the United States custody of the monies brought into the department. As a safeguard, however, the actual accounts were kept by an officer known as the register of the Treasury.

The Bank of the United States aided the Treasury as a repository for federal funds. By the early 1800s, the Bank had become the most influential financial institution in the country. In addition to acting as the federal government's fiscal agent, receiving deposits and making loans to the government, it carried on a regular commercial business, maintaining checking accounts for its customers, financing credit needs, and issuing bank notes (paper money).

The Bank of the United States was also to have a stabilizing effect on the hundreds of other smaller banks across the nation. These local banks were "founded on specie." That is, the capital (the money used or available to the bank for its operations) of the banks was made up largely of gold and silver coins deposited in their vaults. Each bank then loaned money in the form of privately printed bank notes, backed by the gold and silver deposits. Under this system it was fully intended that both depositors and note holders would be able to obtain hard money on demand, simply by presenting the paper money.

During the first half of the 19th century, however, the notes issued by some of these smaller banks did not always bring their full value when cashed at a different bank; notes were accepted at widely varying rates. The private bank notes printed and issued by the larger banks—well known, of reputable standing, and recognized as being able to redeem the notes with hard cash—were usually accepted at face value over a wide area. The notes of less well-known banks, however, were often discounted, some as much as 50 percent. Often the farther the bank notes traveled from the issuing institution, the less their value became. A note of a bank located in Washington, D.C., for

"The Ghost of a Dollar or the Banker's Surprise," a cartoon that mocks the small banks' policies of accepting privately printed bank notes at widely varying rates. Some were discounted as much as 50 percent of the face value.

example, would circulate 40 miles away in Baltimore at 1 or 2 percent less than its face value. That same note 400 miles away in Boston might be cashed in for even less. The simplest transactions thus became complicated by continuing arguments over the amount of payment an individual could obtain on a particular bank note.

The Bank of the United States helped to regulate both the redemption rates and loans of the various state and local banks. The rapid growth of the country in the early decades of the 19th century created a strong demand for bank loans to help build up fledgling industries and commercial enterprises. There was, however, a constant danger that the banks would extend too much credit, thus leading to an economic crisis. The Bank of the United States received a considerable amount of these state banks' notes, accepted by collectors of customs and other Treasury officials on behalf of the federal government, and redeemed them in gold or silver from the issuing institutions. Consequently, the Bank restricted the amount of hard cash available to back up the bank loans. But if the economy appeared to be slowing down, the Bank of the United States could ease up on its redemptions, thus allowing sufficient sums of gold and silver to remain in the state bank vaults to back further loans. The Bank of the United States gradually came to hold a substantial portion of the country's gold and silver money.

When the Bank's 20-year charter neared expiration in 1811, opponents rose up to block its rechartering by Congress. Many Americans felt that the Bank's redemption policies had made it too powerful, at the expense of the smaller state-chartered banks. Some in Congress regarded the Bank as a tool of the old Federalist party. By a narrow vote, the Senate decided not to renew the charter. The Bank wound up its outstanding business and then closed its doors.

The closure of the Bank of the United States could not have come at a more inopportune time for the Treasury Department. The continuing struggle with Great Britain over the rights of American seamen and shipping on the open sea finally erupted into war in 1812. As America mobilized for the ensuing conflict, it soon became apparent that the failure to recharter the Bank of the United States deprived the government of urgently needed financial resources. Finally, during the summer of 1813, with the war in full progress, President James Madison made an appeal before a special session of Congress. The disruption of American commerce, Madison stated, the blockade of ports by British warships, and the decline in customs duties collected from imports forced the nation to seek new means of securing additional funds. Accompanying the president's message was a detailed report from Secretary of the Treasury Albert Gallatin that laid out the measures necessary to acquire the money needed to pursue the war. Under Gallatin's proposal, internal taxes, which Congress had previously been reluctant to establish (partly from fear of creating too large a force of federal tax collectors and prying too closely into the private affairs of individual Americans), would be reinstated. To appease the antitax faction in Congress, Secretary Gallatin proposed that the taxes on liquor, salt, tobacco, and other commodities be regarded only as temporary war measures, in force for no more than one year after the cessation of hostilities. Gallatin also called for a $3 million direct tax on land, dwellings, and slaves, to be collected by the states. Congress approved the measures and, to carry out the new tax laws, created within the Treasury Department an extensive collection agency, headed by the revived office of the commissioner of revenue. The 18 states then in the Union were divided into 191 internal revenue collection districts. Each was staffed by a principal assessor, who determined the amount of tax to be paid, and a collector. Each collector was authorized to appoint as many deputies "as he may think proper" to enforce the new tax laws.

Gallatin remained in Washington for several months, seeing to the arrangements for the war financing. But in February 1814 he resigned his post as secretary of the Treasury to become a member of the commission then attempting to negotiate a settlement with Great Britain. His replacement, George Campbell of Tennessee, was in office for only six months when the British attacked Washington and burned a number of federal buildings to the ground, including the Treasury building. Despite the loss of the headquarters, many of the Treasury's important papers survived the blaze, having been removed from the building prior to the attack. As treasurer of the United States Thomas Tucker related to Congress shortly after the fire, "ledgers, journals, remittances, bank, draft, and other books generally, in use since the year 1810, have been preserved, and many from the first establishment of the Treasury, particularly all the payments and receipts on account of the Treasury, War, and Navy Departments." Most of the books and papers destroyed had been brought from Philadelphia in 1800, and, as Tucker noted, "very few could ever have been wanted."

The War of 1812, however, wreaked more havoc upon the Treasury Department than the mere burning of its building and the loss of old records. The war unraveled many of the economic initiatives of the preceding years. The new taxes enacted by Congress had raised more than $10 million but by no means came close to providing the revenues necessary to continue the war. Congress increased customs duties by 25 percent, but even this measure did not cut significantly into the heavy war debt. Consequently, nearly 90 percent

51

British troops burn the city of Washington in 1814. The Treasury building (to the left of the burning bridge, center) was destroyed by fire, but many of the Treasury's important papers and records had been removed for safekeeping prior to the attack.

of the cost of the war had to be met by heavy government borrowing, with about $80 million in loans and another $37 million in Treasury notes.

The grave financial problems arising from the War of 1812, coupled with the deterioration of the paper currency issued during the war, brought a general suspension of specie (coined money) payment, and emphasized anew the need for a federal banking institution. Shortly before the war's end, in October 1814, Secretary of the Treasury Alexander Dallas recommended to Congress that a Second Bank of the United States be established. Congress concurred and passed legislation to revive the bank's operations. But President Madison vetoed the bill the following year, recalling the arguments that had led to the dismantling of the First Bank. After a year of congressional wrangling, the Second Bank of the United States finally received its charter in 1816.

Like the First Bank of the United States, the Second Bank acted as the nation's central financial institution, serving as a depository for government funds and controlling the quantity of money in circulation. The main office of the bank remained in Philadelphia; in time 25 branches would be established throughout the country. The notes issued by the Second Bank, along with those of its branches, were said to be "good as gold," redeemable for full value anywhere in the United States.

Along with the creation of the Second Bank of the United States came the first federal attempts to examine and regulate the condition of state banks throughout the nation. Both the First and Second Banks were required by charter to submit reports to the Treasury when requested by the secretary. For the most part these reports showed the Bank to be a sound institution. Yet in 1819 the Treasury's examination of the accounts of the Second Bank revealed that the Bank was mismanaged and quickly nearing bankruptcy. As a result, the House of Representatives, concerned over the bank's administration, passed a resolution demanding a closer inquiry into not only the activities of the Second Bank, but those of state banks as well. All state-chartered banks, along with banks in the District of Columbia, were required to submit to the secretary of the Treasury statements revealing various aspects of the banking structure, including their capitalization (the value of the investment of the owner), notes on hand and in circulation, outstanding loans, public and private deposits, and the value of the hard currency in their vaults. Thus began the Treasury's involvement in the examination and regulation of the U.S. banking system. That involvement would be solidified in 1832, when the House passed a resolution formally requiring the secretary of the Treasury to compile for the use of Congress an annual report on the condition of state banks.

The Second Bank of the United States became a central focus of the 1832

Senator Henry Clay of Kentucky actively supported rechartering the Second Bank of the United States and managed to make it a central issue in the 1832 presidential campaign. President Jackson, who was running for reelection, ardently opposed the Bank and vetoed the bank legislation.

presidential campaign, which pitted the incumbent, President Andrew Jackson, against Senator Henry Clay of Kentucky. President Jackson had long been an opponent of the Bank, regarding it as giving too much power to a few rich individuals in the Northeast and hurting the farmers in the South and Midwest. Clay, knowing of Jackson's opposition, made the Bank an issue in the campaign. He used his influence in Congress to get the Bank's charter renewed four years early, thus forcing Jackson to veto the bill. Clay hoped that all those who supported the Bank would be persuaded by this to vote against Jackson in the election. Congress was in an uproar over Jackson's action but failed to override his veto.

The American people ultimately decided the issue of rechartering the Bank when they reelected Jackson by a wide margin. Jackson took his victory as a mandate from the people to do away with the Second Bank of the United States. His principal idea was to withdraw all government deposits, the Bank's lifeblood. Secretary of the Treasury Louis McLane counseled against this strategy. He suggested instead the creation of a new bank, under stricter controls, to replace the Second Bank of the United States. Jackson reorganized

An 1833 cartoon depicts money grabbers running away as President Jackson (second from right) topples the Bank of the United States. By withdrawing funds from the Bank and depositing them in local banks, Jackson hoped to curb the financial power of a small number of wealthy men who he believed were meddling in politics.

55

his cabinet, moving McLane over to the State Department and replacing him with William J. Duane of Pennsylvania. But Duane also opposed removal of the deposits. Jackson, without even notifying Congress, reorganized his cabinet yet again, replacing him with Roger B. Taney. Taney went along with the president's plan. On September 28, 1833, he announced that government funds would no longer be deposited in the Second Bank of the United States and began the transfer of all government funds to state-chartered banks.

Jackson's actions enraged the Senate, which adopted two resolutions censuring both the Treasury Department and the president for exceeding their constitutional powers. In an additional expression of anger, the Senate refused to approve Taney's nomination as secretary of the Treasury. Levi Woodbury of New Hampshire subsequently replaced Taney. (All cabinet posts are created by act of Congress and the nominees for the posts—appointed by the president—require confirmation by the Senate.)

Despite the Senate's reaction, the Second Bank of the United States failed to secure a new charter. In 1836, it relinquished its central banking status and became a state-chartered bank. To fill the void, Congress passed the Deposit Act in 1836, which required the secretary of the Treasury to designate at least one bank in each state and territory as a place of public deposit. These banks then took over the general services previously rendered the federal government by the Bank of the United States.

In 1837 the country found itself in the throes of a crippling financial panic. The overextension of credit by many of the state banks and the reckless speculation in questionable ventures by many individuals caused the national economy to collapse. Unemployment rose and the prices of products soared. Adding fuel to the crisis was President Jackson's directive to the Treasury Department the year before to accept only gold and silver in payment for certain government transactions, in particular the sale of public lands. As a result, many of the hard-currency reserves of the state banks, on which their paper money was based, were quickly diminishing. When the panic struck, many banks, besieged by depositors cashing in paper money for hard currency, failed because of the virtual depletion of gold reserves in their vaults.

The failures of numerous state banks, many of which were the depositories for federal funds, aroused the concern of the new president, Martin Van Buren. In a message before a special session of Congress called to deal with the nation's economic crisis, President Van Buren expressed his fear of continuing to place the public monies in unstable state banks. Instead, he proposed that Congress create a network of independent federal depositories, entrusting the care of all federal funds to Treasury-operated facilities called

A cartoon of the late 1830s shows President Martin Van Buren (second from right) denying to the Bank's ghost any blame for abolishing the Bank. The financial panic of 1837 prompted Van Buren to establish subtreasuries, operated by the Treasury, to help stabilize state banks.

subtreasuries. After three years of political wrangling over the issue, Congress passed the Independent Treasury Act in 1840, establishing subtreasuries in New York City, Boston, Philadelphia, St. Louis, New Orleans, Washington, D.C., and Charleston, South Carolina. The subtreasuries continued to act as the Treasury's major depositories into the first decades of the 20th century.

The banking problem was not the only Treasury Department crisis facing the nation in the 1830s. Tariffs, or the schedules of taxes placed upon imports, were also an explosive issue. Originally, tariffs had been used primarily to generate revenue. During the first decades of the 19th century, however, tariffs had increasingly come to be used as a means of protecting American manufactures from foreign competition. At the urging of factory owners, many from the Northeast, Congress passed the Tariff Act of 1828, resulting in the highest import duties ever levied on European goods.

In the agricultural South, which had few factories and depended on imported goods, many people came to view the high tariffs as inordinately favoring the industrial North. Although tariff rates were reduced somewhat in 1832, political leaders in South Carolina were still not satisfied. On November 24 of that year they called a convention of delegates, elected by the people of South Carolina, to Columbia. The convention passed an Ordinance of Nullification, proclaiming

Senator John C. Calhoun of South Carolina was the guiding hand behind the state legislature's Ordinance of Nullification in 1832. South Carolina declared that the Tariff Act of 1828 was "null, void, and no law, nor binding upon this State, its officers or citizens." The state also forbade Treasury agents to collect customs duties and threatened secession from the Union if the federal government attempted to use force.

that Congress did not have the power to pass a law favoring one section of the country over another and declaring each state's right to reject any unfavorable law passed by Congress. In addition, the southern convention proclaimed that any effort made by Treasury Department officials to collect the duties after February 1, 1833, would cause the state to secede, or withdraw, from the Union.

Treasury officials and customs officers in South Carolina were put in a delicate position. Finally President Jackson, enraged by South Carolina's threat of secession, sent a fleet of seven Treasury revenue cutters and a U.S. Navy warship to Charleston harbor. But in the final hour Senator Henry Clay introduced a bill in Congress to gradually lower the tariff rates over a 10-year period; the move momentarily defused the situation. Congress quickly passed the compromise tariff in 1833, thus averting a head-on conflict and staying for the time the secession question.

The Treasury's year of trial, however, was not yet over. That same year, in 1833, the main Treasury building in Washington, D.C., constructed after the British burning of Washington in 1814, was destroyed by fire. But this time the Treasury Department suffered a considerable loss. Nearly all the records and correspondence of the secretary of the Treasury, from the establishment of the department to the time of the fire, were destroyed. An investigation into the cause of the fire eventually led to the arrest of two brothers, who were charged with setting the fire in an attempt to destroy certain papers that would prove fraudulent conduct by a number of Treasury agents. One brother was finally acquitted, but the other was sentenced to 10 years in prison.

The next three years found the department working out of temporary quarters. In 1836, Congress finally passed legislation to begin construction of a new "fireproof building of such dimensions as may be required for the present and future accommodations" of the Treasury Department. Originally, the plan called for placing the new Treasury building on the old site so as not to obstruct the view of the Capitol enjoyed from the east wing of the White House. But months stretched into years as site planners and architects argued over how best to lay out the building on the construction site. Finally President Jackson, growing impatient with the delays, walked out of the adjacent White House one morning to see for himself the vacant site of the old Treasury building. Jackson surveyed the empty lot, and then, in a grand gesture, drove his walking stick into the ground near the northeast corner of the lot, proclaiming "Right here is where I want the cornerstone laid!" The architect of the building, Robert Mills, would later verify the story, testifying before a congressional committee that

Construction of the Department of the Treasury building in 1862. The Treasury building and most of its records were destroyed by a fire in 1833; President Jackson personally selected the site for the new "fireproof" building, which underwent a number of building phases from 1836 to 1869.

the precise location of the cornerstone of the building had been determined by the "positive directions of the President."

The Treasury Department's new headquarters was completed in 1842. The 150 rooms inside the expansive granite building, however, soon proved inadequate to house the growing executive staff of the department. Within a few years Treasury officials were back before Congress petitioning for funds to enlarge the building, and in 1855 Congress granted the department permission to do so. A massive, colonnaded south wing was just nearing completion in 1861 when war erupted between the North and the South, temporarily halting further construction.

The Civil War would not only affect the Treasury's building plans; the war would also radically alter its duties. At first, the federal government planned to finance the war against the Confederacy with borrowed money. Accordingly, Congress authorized the secretary of the Treasury to begin issuing securities (bonds and bills) to raise the needed funds. Toward that end, Secretary Salmon P. Chase established a Division of Loans within the Treasury Department. But it soon became apparent that the loans by themselves would not be sufficient to fund what promised to be a long struggle. Customs duties had declined precipitously, due in part to the department's loss of the Southern ports. Those ports were now regulated by the Confederacy's own treasury department, and Southern customs officers collected import duties to finance the Southern war effort. The blockading of Southern ports by Union warships, however, would have a severe impact on the amount of customs revenues flowing into the Confederacy's coffers.

Union gunboats capture a Confederate blockade-runner during the Civil War. Customs duties declined abruptly during the war, partly because the Treasury could no longer collect taxes from Southern ports, which were regulated by the Confederacy's own treasury department. Union warships blockaded the Southern ports to stop the flow of revenue into the Confederacy's treasury.

As the war dragged on into the spring of 1862, Congress wrestled with the problem of how best to finance it. The public debt was increasing at a rate of $2 million a day; customs duties were still in sharp decline, and internal revenue measures enacted in a special session the previous summer were inadequate. Congress responded to the crisis by passing the Internal Revenue Act. Signed into law by President Abraham Lincoln on July 1, 1862, the sweeping revenue-producing law placed taxes on a wide range of items, such as spirits, tobacco, advertisements, medicines, perfumes, cosmetics, and playing cards. It also placed a tax on licenses to operate businesses such as insurance companies, banks, and public utilities.

But perhaps the single most important measure included in the act was the creation of the nation's first income tax. The tax was to be "progressive"; that is, the amount would vary with the level of income. The measure levied a tax of 3 percent on annual incomes between $600 and $10,000 and a tax of 5 percent on any income above $10,000.

Under the terms of the Internal Revenue Act, the president was directed to divide the country into collection districts and to appoint, with the advice and consent of the Senate, an assessor and a collector for each district. The assessor was to travel through the district to prepare assessment lists that would then be delivered to the tax collector. These lists would constitute the collector's warrant to seek payment for the taxes owed the federal government. The entire collection organization was placed under the direction of a commissioner of internal revenue; in 1862, President Lincoln appointed George Boutwell, a former governor of Massachusetts, as the first commissioner.

Immediately upon taking office, Boutwell began the complicated task of organizing the administrative staff and field officers necessary to begin tax collection. In 1862, however, Americans were not accustomed to the idea of paying taxes. Collecting the taxes on spirits and liquor proved especially difficult and at times hazardous. Untaxed stills hidden in remote parts of the country and guarded by rifle-toting moonshiners (the operators of the illegal stills) deprived the government of much-needed income to outfit the army. In 1863, Commissioner Boutwell began hiring detectives to combat the illegal production of whiskey.

Despite the risks and hardships of tax collection, the internal revenue measures added considerably to the federal revenue. After the end of the first full year of collection, 1864, income taxes had contributed more than $20 million to the Treasury. The tax on manufactures and products yielded more than $36 million, with the distilled spirits tax adding more than $30 million. Within 2 years, receipts from internal revenue, collected by a staff of 4,400 employees, would reach $311 million. Even though this was a sizable sum, the federal government still had to rely on borrowing to finance 80 percent of the war costs.

Another measure proposed by Secretary Chase and approved by Congress to help pay for wartime operations was the issue of the government's own paper money. Unlike other notes, these U.S. notes were not founded on specie and could not be exchanged for gold and silver coins. Ultimately, however, like the paper money of the revolutionary war period, the value of these federal notes would decrease sharply as more and more of them were issued.

In 1862, the department installed printing presses in the basement of the Treasury building, and a small staff of two men and four women began overprinting the Treasury seal (which depicts a shield bearing a balance and a key) and the signatures of the register of the Treasury and the treasurer of the United States on $1 and $2 notes printed by private bank note companies. The overprinting served as evidence that the notes were lawfully issued by the federal government. Spencer Clark, then chief of the Treasury's Bureau of Construction, was placed in charge of the basement printing operation.

Soon after taking charge, however, Clark became troubled by the high prices charged the government by the private bank note companies contracted to print the currency notes. He suggested to Secretary Chase that the Treasury itself could produce the notes "for a comparatively small outlay, at a great saving of cost." Chase put the proposition before Congress, which concurred, and in 1863 the Treasury Department began printing its own paper money for the first time.

To safeguard the currency against counterfeiters (people who make fake money, intending to pass it off as genuine), a special paper was developed. Its secret manufacturing process was known only to those immediately engaged by the Treasury Department to produce the paper. As an extra precaution, the machinery necessary to manufacture the paper was installed in the Treasury building and kept under guard. Special inks were developed for the printing of the notes and the department decided to use two colors to make the bills harder to counterfeit. But ordinary ink, when printed on the back of the notes, had a tendency to bleed through to the opposite side, blurring the printing on the front. Consequently, a special shade of green was developed for printing the backs of the notes, making the back printing less noticeable; the fronts of

A dollar bill, called a greenback, 1862. The Treasury Department began to overprint the Treasury seal and the signatures of the register and treasurer on $1 and $2 notes, which were originally printed by private companies contracted by the government. The Treasury did not begin printing its own paper money until 1863.

the notes, meanwhile, were printed with black ink. These notes became known as "greenbacks."

As the Civil War progressed, many citizens, fearing the worst, began hoarding their hard cash, removing thousands of dollars in coins from circulation every day. In New York City, one house was said to have collapsed from the weight of gold and silver coins inside. To replace the small coins rapidly disappearing from circulation, Secretary Chase reported to Congress in 1863 that there was "a manifest necessity for fractional currency authorized by the national government." Congress agreed and directed the Treasury to begin the printing of small denomination notes. Once in production, however, the fractional paper currency became a controversial issue. As to the smallest note issued by the department, a three-cent note, some in Congress expressed doubt as to the actual need for so low a denomination. Another fractional note that caused some concern at the Capitol was the five-cent note; to Congress's surprise, the note bore the portrait of Spencer Clark, the superintendent of the Treasury Department's printing operations. The dispute eventually led Congress to pass a law in 1863 prohibiting the use of a portrait of any living person on any security issued by the United States; that law remains in effect today.

In addition to the production of paper money, the Treasury during the Civil War also began printing its own revenue stamps. These were affixed to objects subject to internal revenue and denoted that the tax had been paid. Medicines, playing cards, tobacco products, liquor, beer, and other products were sealed with a variety of tax stamps.

The demands placed on the Treasury by the increased revenue needs of the Civil War, and in particular by the department's expanding printing operations, led to an unprecedented growth in the number of employees filling the offices of the main Treasury building in Washington. At the war's start the Treasury Department employed 380 clerks. Within three years, the number had risen to more than 2,000. Because continuing army enlistments created a wartime shortage of men, the great majority of these new Treasury workers were women; they were, in fact, the first significant group of women employed by the federal government.

To regulate the distribution of the new national bank notes rolling off the Treasury presses, in 1863 Congress passed the Currency Act, placing the operation under the control of the new Office of the Comptroller of the Currency. Under the act, associations of individuals could be authorized by the comptroller to establish national banks in their cities and towns, to buy federal securities,

The five-cent note bearing the portrait of Spencer Clark, superintendent of the Treasury's printing operations. In 1863, Congress passed a law forbidding the use of a portrait of any living person on government-issued securities.

to receive interest from the government on its holdings, and to issue the national bills distributed to the banks through the comptroller's office.

Despite the urgent need of the federal government to recruit banks to its new national banking system, the first comptroller of the currency, Hugh McCulloch, appointed by President Lincoln in 1863, moved cautiously in approving applications. Information on the experience of the bank's organizers in financial matters, their ability and character, the economic forecast for the bank's location, and the other banking facilities already available in the area, were required before an application would be approved. By November 1863, Comptroller McCulloch reported to Congress that 134 national banks had been organized, with nearly 60 percent of them operating in only 4 Northern states: New York, Pennsylvania, Ohio, and Indiana. The following December, the first of the Treasury's bank notes were distributed for circulation.

The Currency Act of 1863 was amended the following year by the National Bank Act, which required the comptroller of the currency to examine regularly the records of the national banks in order to ensure sound management and to expose any "improper practices on the part of bankers, and violations of the provisions of the law." The Treasury hired a corps of bank examiners to enforce the act and sent it out into the field. If the examiners turned up continuing infractions by a national bank, the comptroller was empowered to revoke its charter.

Not all state banks, however, chose to become national banks. Many preferred to operate under the looser regulations of the states. As a means of encouraging the banks to come under the national system, Secretary Chase, along with Comptroller McCulloch, recommended to Congress that a high federal tax be imposed on the bank notes issued by the state-chartered institutions. In 1865, Congress levied a 10 percent tax on state bank notes; within a year, more than half of the state-chartered banks switched over to the federal system. By 1866, some 1,600 institutions had joined the national banking system and were distributing federal greenbacks.

Despite the safeguards against counterfeiting, however, those greenbacks soon fell victim to unscrupulous individuals churning out fake money. So many bogus federal bills found their way into circulation that the Treasury Department was forced to institute measures to protect its paper money. In 1865, the Secret Service was created within the department for the express purpose of investigating and arresting persons suspected of counterfeiting. Agents fanned out across the country, eventually arresting hundreds of counterfeiters and greatly reducing the number of fraudulent bills in circulation.

66

After the end of the Civil War in 1865, many of the Treasury programs created to finance the conflict were slowly phased out. Although internal taxes on alcohol and tobacco continued to be assessed and collected, the income tax was gradually reduced after public protest. Finally, in 1872, the income tax was abolished; once again, the bulk of the federal revenue would be derived from customs duties.

Nebraskan settlers in front of their sod home in 1887. As American families pushed westward and expanded the nation's borders, the Treasury Department increased its influence in the western territories by collecting tariffs and overseeing the sale of public lands.

FOUR

A Period of Readjustment, 1872–1945

In the second half of the 19th century America entered an era of tremendous growth. It was a nation on the move, expanding its borders and linking the oceans; it was a nation coming of age as a world power. Treasury officials often accompanied the settlers pushing westward, establishing a federal presence in the newly opened territories and enforcing the various federal laws relating to revenue, immigration, and smuggling. By the century's end, customs officers, once assigned to only 2,000 miles of Atlantic shore, were patrolling more than 20,000 miles of coast and border.

As the western towns and cities matured, however, they began to look upon the tariffs enforced by the customs officers with some suspicion. During the Civil War, tariffs had been steadily increased to finance the Union war effort. After the conflict's end, however, tariffs, unlike other federal taxes, remained high. Northern manufacturing interests wanted high protective tariffs in order to limit competition from foreign manufacturers and assure themselves of steady profits for their own products. Farmers in the Midwest and West, however, saw the high tariffs as unfairly protecting big business and imposing higher prices upon the products they had to buy to keep their farms going. Growing pressure from the farmers brought about a nominal reduction in tariffs

An 1888 cartoon shows American labor groups' dissatisfaction with President Cleveland's trade policy. Despite increased import and export activities, including the collection of customs duties, many laborers were upset by the foreign competition. John Bull (left), a symbol of Great Britain, personifies the locomotive that the United States decided to import from Britain because it was cheaper to buy ready-made than to construct in America's outmoded factories.

in 1872, but an ensuing financial panic and economic depression cut so deeply into federal revenues that within three years the import taxes were again raised. With prosperity's return in the 1880s, exports and imports rose sharply, bringing in customs duties in record amounts and creating a $100 million surplus in the Treasury. Despite the surplus, no significant reduction in the tariffs followed. In fact, by the end of the century, customs duties—in the name of protectionism—would rise to their highest rates since the Civil War.

Compounding the controversies swirling around the Treasury Department during the late 19th century would be the issue of the nation's gold and silver supplies. The discovery of new gold and silver deposits in the western lands during the period expanded the Treasury's responsibilities. The first significant discovery, which led to the California gold rush of the late 1840s and 1850s, produced more gold than the U.S. Mint in Philadelphia could handle. Moreover, shipping the gold across the country proved both risky and time consuming.

Consequently, in 1854, a branch mint was established in San Francisco, California, along with an assay office where gold was measured, weighed, bought, and disbursed, and paper money redeemed for specie. (Assay offices tested the precious-metal content of samples but did not coin money.) In 1870, another branch mint was opened in Carson City, Nevada, following the discovery of huge silver deposits in the area; other mints followed in New Orleans, Louisiana, and Denver, Colorado. As a result of the growth, in 1873, after nearly 75 years of operating as an independent agency, the U.S. Mint formally became a part of the Treasury Department.

In the same year, however, the federal government stopped minting silver coins. Congress, noting that only about 8 million silver dollars had been minted

A mining camp at Mount Shasta, California, in 1849. In 1854, the Treasury established a branch mint in San Francisco because of the high risk of robbery in shipping gold east to Philadelphia.

in the previous 80 years, decided that there was little need for that coin, and consequently dropped the silver dollar from the list of coins produced by the U.S. Mint. At the same time, the amount of greenbacks in circulation was dwindling, from a postwar high of some $400 million to around $300 million. Rapid economic development was making serious demands on the country's financial resources. Huge sums of money were sought to finance the unprecedented amount of new construction going on in the numerous communities springing up throughout the Midwest and West. But when currency was in short supply, development was stifled. Those people who wanted more money in circulation, called "inflationists," were incensed at the apparent failure of the Treasury Department to increase the nation's flow of cash. (Inflation is the increase in the volume of money beyond the proportion of available goods, resulting in a rise in price levels.) In 1874, Congress responded to the call for more money and authorized the printing of enough paper money to bring the total back up to $400 million. But President Ulysses S. Grant vetoed the bill. Grant pressed Congress for a new bill and got his wish in 1875. The new bill required the Treasury to resume the redemption of paper dollars in specie by January 1, 1879, thus returning the nation to a currency based on metallic value nearly two decades after its suspension during the Civil War. Although the department could have redeemed the paper money in either gold or silver, the act directed it to pay only in gold coins, thus putting the nation unofficially and exclusively on a gold standard.

In the 1870s, in opposition to the government's new policy, there arose a political group, backed by the silver-mining interests of the West, that clamored for a return to the nation's original two-metal standard of gold and silver. Campaigning under the banner of "free silver," the group pushed for the Treasury to resume minting as many silver coins as possible, thus increasing the amount of money in circulation. The free-silver forces eventually found a political ally in the emerging Greenback party, organized primarily by farmers who similarly campaigned for an increased issue of paper money. Both held to the basic conviction that the prices they received for farm products remained low because not enough money was in circulation. If, on the other hand, the government issued more money, consumers could purchase more farm goods, and with the rising demand would come a rise in farm prices.

The Greenback party enjoyed little political success and eventually disbanded. Congress made some concessions to the free-silver advocates in 1878 and 1890, when it directed the Treasury to purchase some $156 million worth of silver with the intention of minting (coining) it. But the agreements to buy silver were repealed in 1893 when the nation's gold reserves, used to buy the silver, got dangerously low, causing a run on the federal Treasury and a temporary suspension of the issuance of gold-redeemable notes.

The national fight over the federal government's management of the national money supply came to a head in the presidential election of 1896, when the gold-standard Republicans squared off against the free-silver Democrats. At the contest's end, the Republican candidate, William McKinley, emerged victorious. Backed by Congress, McKinley put the issue to rest in 1900 with the passage of the Gold Standard Act, which officially made gold the base for all money in the United States.

President McKinley's strong stand on the nation's finances helped earn him reelection in 1900. But McKinley's second term was to be tragically brief: The following year the president was assassinated while attending the Pan American Exposition in Buffalo, New York. His vice-president, Theodore Roosevelt, assumed the presidency. McKinley's assassination raised serious questions and concerns about the safety of the president. To provide himself protection, President Roosevelt turned to the one enforcement arm of the federal

During the 1896 presidential election campaign, Democrat William Jennings Bryan (left) represented the interests of the American farmer and laborer with his free-silver platform, which urged the return of the nation's two-metal standard of gold and silver. Republican William McKinley (right) represented the businessman with his gold-standard platform, which promoted gold as the base for all U.S. money. McKinley won the election.

Customs officials perform standard health checks on immigrants at Ellis Island in New York in the early 1900s. The Customs Service regulated products and people coming through American ports and crossing borders, to protect U.S. public health and agriculture.

government on hand in the nation's capital: the Treasury's Secret Service. Beginning in 1901, Secret Service agents accompanied the president wherever he went. Congress would eventually pass formal legislation authorizing presidential protection by the Secret Service in 1906. In 1917, protection would be extended to members of the president's immediate family.

As America emerged as a world power at the turn of the century, the Treasury's responsibility for regulating the flood of people and products through the nation's ports grew enormously. Congress enacted new laws to protect environmental interests and the quality of life and to safeguard American agriculture, business, and public health. To enforce these new laws Congress turned to the Customs Service. The Customs Service still attended to the principal business of enforcing the tariff laws and assessing and collecting duties. But now customs officers found themselves thrust into a new role. In 1881 they began enforcing the Trademark Act, which prohibited the importation of manufactured items that were fraudulent copies of U.S. trademarked items. (A trademark is a name, mark, or symbol used by a manufacturer to identify a product to the consumer. For example, George Eastman used Kodak as the trademark for the cameras he produced.) In 1891, the Customs Service began enforcing the International Copyright Act, passed by Congress to protect American authors from piracy by foreign publishers and extending similar rights to foreign authors whose books were published in America. (Today the Copyright Office issues copyrights, granting the exclusive right to reproduce, publish, and sell the creative products of authors, composers, artists, etc.)

In 1909, the Customs Service was charged with enforcing the Lacy Act, which prohibited the importation of slaughtered game birds and waterfowl, made necessary by the wide and sometimes outrageous use of feathers in the fashions of the time. The act also prohibited the importation of mongoose, fruit bats, sparrows, starlings, and other animals that destroyed farmers' crops. In the same year the Customs Service began enforcing the nation's first Narcotic Prohibition Act, which made it "unlawful to import into the United States opium in any form or any preparation or derivative thereof." Later prohibitions against the importation of cocaine and marijuana would follow, and they would also be enforced by the service.

The operations of the Treasury's Bureau of Engraving and Printing also expanded. In 1894, the bureau began printing all U.S. postage stamps, a duty previously performed by private printing companies. In the bureau's first year of operation more than 21 million sheets of stamps rolled off the Treasury presses.

At the turn of the century the department's Bureau of Internal Revenue found its role once again enlarged. Populist reformers (mostly western and southern agricultural groups) had begun campaigning in the 1890s for the resurrection of the income tax as a just means of spreading out the revenue burden. In 1894, as part of a tariff reduction act, Congress acquiesced in the enactment of a 2 percent tax on personal incomes above $2,000. Accordingly, an Income Tax Division was revived within the Treasury Department. The following year, however, the Supreme Court ruled the tax unconstitutional on the grounds that it was a direct tax and not apportioned among the states on the basis of population, as prescribed in the Constitution. The Treasury's Income Tax Division was promptly disbanded.

75

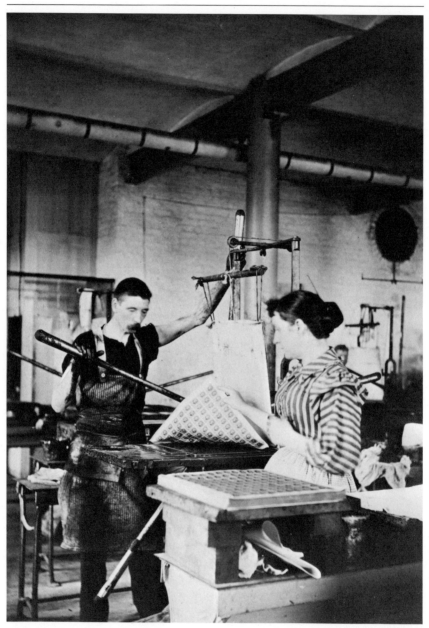

Two employees of the Bureau of Engraving and Printing print and stack sheets of postage stamps in 1904. Prior to 1904 the Treasury Department contracted private companies to print stamps.

A Puck *magazine cover of 1895 aptly illustrates the unpopularity and eventual failure of the Treasury's income tax measures. Despite initial support from Populist reformers, the two percent income tax passed by Congress in 1894 was declared unconstitutional by the Supreme Court in the following year.*

The pressure for personal and corporate income taxes based on the ability to pay continued to build. In 1909, Congress levied a 2 percent excise tax on net corporate income above $5,000. (Net corporate income is a company's earnings minus its expenses.)

Meanwhile, the Sixteenth Amendment to the Constitution, calling for the creation of an income tax, slowly made its way through the ratification process, which required the consent of three fourths of the states. In 1913, when Wyoming became the 36th state to ratify the document, the income tax amendment finally became part of the Constitution. From then on, Congress was granted "the power to lay and collect taxes on incomes, from whatever source derived, without apportionment among the several states, and without regard to any census or enumeration."

With the potential for increased revenues thus in hand, Congress convened in a special session to revise the tariff laws. It enacted the lowest tariffs since the Civil War, reducing duties on nearly 1,000 items and placing more than 100 other items on the import-free list. Attached to the tariff law was a graduated income tax that levied a 1 percent tax on net personal incomes above $3,000, with a surtax of up to 6 percent on incomes of more than $50,000. The tariff act also repealed the corporation tax of 1909 and imposed a new tax on net incomes of corporations. To administer the new income tax laws the Treasury Department once again created a personal income tax division within the Bureau of Internal Revenue. Some 3,700 employees worked in the field and more than 250 worked at the Washington headquarters to process the income tax returns.

Also in 1913, Congress passed the Federal Reserve Act, significantly restructuring the nation's banking system. The act created 12 banking districts within the United States, each with a Federal Reserve Bank to assist the banks in its district and to distribute coin and currency from the Federal Reserve System. The 12 Federal Reserve Banks were empowered to issue a new type of paper money brought into being by the act: the Federal Reserve note. Control of the provisions of the act was placed in a presidentially appointed Federal Reserve Board, an independent federal agency that was to work in conjunction with the Treasury Department. The new national banking system was intended to adjust the nation's money supply, eliminating the occurrences of money shortages by periodically releasing the amounts necessary to match the public need. Initially, the Congress had intended the Federal Reserve notes, printed by the Treasury and first released into circulation in 1914, to form only a small part of the money then in circulation. By 1920, however, the total value of Federal Reserve notes in daily use exceeded that of all other notes and bills. With the establishment of the Federal Reserve System also came the abolition of the older network of subtreasuries, in use since the 1840s.

Just as America was readjusting its revenue, banking, and currency systems, war erupted in Europe in 1914, sending the international economy into a spin. German warships cruising the Atlantic Ocean threatened and, at times, attacked American merchant ships and their crews, crippling commerce. In 1914 the Treasury Department established a Bureau of War Risk Insurance, providing up to $5 million of insurance for American ships at sea. Regardless, imports to the United States declined drastically; coupled with the reduction in the tariff rates, income from customs duties decreased substantially since 1912. The new income tax system was up and running, but, when the United

The first Federal Reserve Board in 1914. Congress passed the Federal Reserve Act of 1913 establishing the Federal Reserve System, a national banking system, to help the Treasury regulate the U.S. money supply.

States was drawn into the conflict in 1917, increased revenues were needed to finance the war effort. Congress's formal declaration of war was accompanied by the passage of the War Revenue Act, a sweeping measure calling for increases in a variety of taxes, including those imposed on personal incomes, beverages, tobacco, public utilities, and insurance companies. Even greater increases were to follow. By 1918, the income tax provisions included a rate structure reaching up to 77 percent, and for the first time the internal taxes collected by the Treasury exceeded the billion-dollar mark; by the year's end, the department had collected more than $3 billion.

The increased tax revenues, however, were to pay for only a fraction of the war's cost, which by 1918 had reached over $41 billion. Once again the government was forced to borrow. The Treasury Department administered one borrowing program—the issuance of war bonds, known as Liberty Loans. These bonds were sold at a discount and could be redeemed at face value after a specified number of years; if the bonds were cashed in before maturity the seller might receive as little as 82 cents on the dollar. In all, the department

IOSEPH PENNELL DEL.

THAT LIBERTY SHALL NOT PERISH FROM THE EARTH BUY LIBERTY BONDS
FOURTH LIBERTY LOAN

This 1918 poster showing the destruction of the Statue of Liberty brought the threat of world war home to Americans, encouraging them to finance the war effort by buying Liberty Bonds. Liberty Bonds provided the Treasury with hard cash and a profit for the holder when the bond was redeemed.

staged five bond drives, raising a total of $21 billion for the war effort. The response by the American people was overwhelming; in the fourth drive, nearly 22 million citizens, or more than one fifth of the total population, purchased bonds.

The demand for war bonds and other war-finance programs brought with it a significant increase in the Treasury work force. The department's Bureau of Engraving and Printing, for example, had almost 9,000 employees by the war's end in 1918. Similarly, the Bureau of Internal Revenue increased its personnel to nearly 20,000 to handle its growing revenue collection and processing responsibilities. The escalating government borrowing during the war led the Treasury to consolidate and expand several of the agencies charged with managing the national debt. They were brought together under the Public Debt Service, headed by a commissioner of the public debt.

Once again the urgencies of war financing had brought substantial changes to the Treasury Department. Immediately following World War I, peacetime legislation brought new challenges to the department. In 1919, the states ratified the Eighteenth Amendment to the Constitution—known as the Prohibition amendment—making it unlawful to manufacture, sell, or transport intoxicating liquors in the United States. That same year Congress passed the National Prohibition Enforcement Act, also known as the Volstead Act, charging the Treasury Department with the responsibility for tracking down and arresting those who violated the new liquor laws.

To handle the increased duties, the Bureau of Internal Revenue set up a prohibition unit. One section of the unit was involved with the enforcement and regulatory provisions of the act; a second section supervised the issuance of permits for the legitimate and approved manufacture of alcohol for medicinal, industrial, or religious purposes. Trafficking in illegal liquor—whether rum-running, bootlegging, or moonshining—soon became big business in America, dominated by racketeers and mob syndicates. In 1925 alone, more than 3,700 Internal Revenue agents made some 77,000 arrests under the Volstead Act, seizing more than $11 million in property. While Internal Revenue agents scoured the U.S. interior, customs agents were busy along the nation's coasts and borders trying to stop the flow of smuggled liquor. The work proved dangerous; some 40 customs agents lost their lives battling rumrunners.

In 1927, the duties of the Treasury's prohibition unit were turned over to the Justice Department. With the repeal of Prohibition in 1933, however, the manufacture and sale of alcohol once again became legal. The enforcement of federal liquor laws and the relevant tax collection responsibilities were returned to the Treasury Department.

81

In 1922, in Washington, D.C., members of the IRS's prohibition unit pose with a 500-gallon still they confiscated. The Treasury Department enforced the Eighteenth Amendment, which prohibited the sale, transportation, and consumption of alcohol in the United States from 1919 to 1933.

In 1925, at the same time that Treasury agents were wrestling with Prohibition violators, a special committee appointed by Secretary of the Treasury Andrew Mellon struggled with the less threatening question of currency size. Many Americans had begun to complain that the oversized paper currency (7½ in. x 3½ in.) was too cumbersome for daily use. As a result, the Treasury committee (a committee of congressmen and Treasury officials brought together by Secretary Mellon) recommended replacing the larger bills then in circulation with smaller, unified notes, each to bear the portrait of an important figure in American history. For the new $1 bill, the committee recommended George Washington's portrait, reasoning that as that denomination of bills had the greatest circulation it should bear the likeness of the most familiar American president. For the $5 bill, the committee suggested Abraham Lincoln's portrait. The committee's recommendations, including suggested portraits for the higher denominations of bills, were approved by Secretary Mellon in 1927 and formed the basis for the paper currency designs still in use in the United States.

The new notes began to circulate in July 1929. Ironically, within three months of the new bills' appearance, the stock market crashed, signaling the beginning of a catastrophic economic depression and starting a chain of events that led to changes at the Treasury Department. Many stock buyers had purchased stocks on credit, using up cash reserves to pay their brokers when those stocks lost their value and they wanted to sell. The urgent need for cash put pressure on the banks. The Federal Reserve System was unable to increase the money supply in time to stave off the crisis. Plunges in commodity prices (the prices of agricultural and mining products, for example) soon followed; individual and corporate incomes collapsed. By January 1930, nearly 4 million Americans found themselves unemployed; by the year's end, more than 1,300 banks had closed their doors on depositors.

The Treasury, which through the postwar years of the 1920s had enjoyed an era of budget surpluses, now found its own reserves dwindling. Federal revenues also fell off sharply as the nation's income decreased. By 1932, the department's revenue collections amounted to only $1.5 billion, the lowest total since World War I. And yet, despite the alarming decline in revenues, the public looked to the government with increasing intensity to do something to pull the nation out of the crisis. Somewhat belatedly, in 1932 Congress began passing a series of acts authorizing loans to the states for relief purposes, to be financed by the issue of bonds. But the depression continued to deepen daily. President Herbert Hoover, under whose administration the crisis began, gradually lost the confidence of the American people, and the 1932 election was a landslide victory for Franklin D. Roosevelt.

Roosevelt took the presidential oath of office in 1933, when the nation was economically and socially coming apart at the seams. Unemployment continued to climb and national banks continued to close as a seemingly endless stream of depositors redeemed paper money for gold, seriously depleting the nation's reserve. Just one day after his inauguration, Roosevelt issued a proclamation declaring a four-day nationwide "bank holiday," bringing a halt to all banking operations, placing a ban on the export of all gold, silver, and currency, and effectively stopping the panic-stricken run on the banks. The comptroller of the currency and the Federal Reserve Board worked together to ensure that only those banks found to be in sound financial order would be allowed to reopen.

Later in 1933, Roosevelt took all U.S. currency off the gold standard in an effort to make more money available and thereby stimulate the depressed economy. That same year the production of gold coins by the U.S. Mint stopped, and all gold coins were removed from circulation. In 1934, in a further effort to control the wildly fluctuating value of the dollar, Congress passed the

Business was brisk at the New York Stock Exchange on October 24, 1929, when almost 13 million shares of stock were sold. The following Tuesday the stock market crashed, signaling the start of a massive economic depression that would lead to many changes in the Treasury Department.

A Dubuque, Iowa, couple outside their shack home in 1940. Despite President Franklin D. Roosevelt's recovery programs and the Treasury's efforts to raise revenues for the programs through an increase in corporate, income, and excise taxes the mood of the nation remained somber.

Gold Reserve Act, calling for all gold remaining in Federal Reserve Banks to be transferred to the Treasury. To store the gold reserves, the Treasury Department constructed the Fort Knox Bullion Depository at the Fort Knox army base in Kentucky. (Bullion is uncoined gold or silver in bar form.) Completed in 1937, the impregnable granite, steel, and concrete building contained a two-level steel vault to hold bars of gold produced by the U.S. Mint and bars made from melted gold coins removed from circulation. The gold was sealed in the vault by a door weighing more than 20 tons.

President Roosevelt's recovery programs, known collectively as the New Deal, included federal job programs such as the Civilian Conservation Corps, in which young men were employed to plant trees, build roads, and construct dams throughout the nation. To advance his relief programs, Roosevelt requested $10.5 billion from Congress. This was a substantial appropriation that required additional financing measures. Consequently, Congress increased tax rates and authorized a variety of levies to generate revenue. Another Treasury measure designed to support the government's depression recovery programs was the issuance of small-denomination bonds, called "baby bonds," in 1935. These affordable bonds were intended to encourage the participation of average citizens in financing the government's program. They were the first true savings bond offered by the Treasury Department. President Roosevelt kicked off the sales campaign by purchasing the first bond at a White House ceremony. Over the next 5 years nearly 2 million Americans would buy more than 11 million bonds (representing $3 billion).

Although Roosevelt's various recovery programs brought a renewed confidence in the U.S. economy and to some degree eased the depression, they did not bring an end to the nation's financial woes. What brought the country out of its economic slump was, tragically, the outbreak of World War II. In 1941, with the conflict raging across Europe, the United States began to increase defense expenditures to bring aid to its beleaguered overseas allies. Following the Japanese bombing of the U.S. naval base in Pearl Harbor, Hawaii, in December 1941, the massive defense needs of the nation once again brought about a restructuring of the Treasury Department's revenue programs. Congress raised income taxes sharply, moving them from a relatively narrow base to one affecting millions of Americans. Congress also raised corporate taxes and increased many excise taxes. As a result, the Internal Revenue Service's workforce grew from 27,000 in 1941 to more than 50,000 in 1945.

Yet, as in World War I, the amount of tax revenues collected by the Treasury Department fell short of covering the war costs. The government was forced to borrow heavily. One such measure involved the expansion of the

President Roosevelt signs a declaration of war against Japan on December 8, 1941, formalizing the United States's entrance into World War II. The outbreak of the war created new defense-related jobs, such as building ships and producing munitions, and helped to revive the nation's economy.

In 1943, a worker in a Baltimore, Maryland, shipyard shows off his newly purchased war bond. The Treasury established the War Savings Bonds program to help the government meet its tremendous war expenses. During World War II, Americans purchased more than $156 billion worth of War Savings Bonds and Savings Stamps.

department's savings bonds program. Defense Bonds, later called War Savings Bonds, replaced the baby bonds issued during the depression. The Treasury set up a War Savings Staff to administer the program, and a nationwide network of volunteers enlisted to promote sale. Banks served as voluntary agents; community leaders organized bond sales committees; employers encouraged bond purchases through payroll savings plans; and a galaxy of movie stars, musicians, and celebrities joined publicity campaigns to boost bond sales.

Also stimulating the sale of war bonds was the Treasury's Savings Stamp program. Buyers could purchase the stamps in 10-cent, 25-cent, $1, or $5 denominations. When purchasers had saved $18.75 worth of stamps, they could exchange them for a $25 bond. Between 1941, when the stamps were first offered, and 1946, the Treasury's Bureau of Engraving and Printing printed more than 8 billion Savings Stamps, carrying a value of more than $1.7 billion. During the war, Americans purchased more than $156 billion worth of Savings Stamps and War Savings Bonds, significantly contributing to the Treasury Department's—and the nation's—war-financing efforts.

A Customs Service agent uses a dog, specially trained to sniff out drugs, to inspect a cargo area in an airplane. The Treasury Department has used detector dogs to help combat drug smugglers since 1970.

FIVE

The Treasury's Structure in the Modern Era

In the decades after World War II, the United States entered a period of extended economic prosperity. The Treasury Department continued to enlarge its own operations to keep pace with the demands of an increasingly complex economy. Today, with more than 120,000 employees and an annual budget exceeding $100 billion, the Treasury Department is among the largest of the government's nonmilitary departments. And in the 1980s, as in the 1780s, the rest of the government looks to the Treasury Department to secure the funds to keep it functioning properly.

Through the years, a number of lesser fiscal responsibilities originally assigned to the Treasury Department were gradually transferred to other departments. The Revenue Cutter Service and the Lifesaving Service, for example, both initially under the Treasury's control, were combined in 1915 to form the U.S. Coast Guard and eventually moved to the Department of Transportation in 1967. The Public Health Service took over the operation of the nation's marine hospitals (federal hospitals for American seamen), at one time supervised by the collectors of customs. The Immigration and Naturalization Service took over the control of immigrants from the Customs Service in 1891. The Office of the Supervising Architect of the Treasury, once responsible for the construction of all federal buildings, was moved in 1939 to the Federal Works Agency, becoming in 1949 an independent agency, the General Services Administration. And in 1968 the Justice Department took over the Treasury Department's Bureau of Narcotics, which became the Drug Enforcement Administration.

Despite the shifting of programs inside and outside of the department, many of the main functions and offices of the Treasury remain essentially the same today as in 1789. At the head of the department is the secretary of the Treasury, appointed by the president with the advice and consent of the Senate. The secretary has the dual responsibility of determining the proper financial policies of the government and the proper way to administer those policies within the department. As the primary financial adviser to the president, the secretary assumes an active and vital role in formulating and recommending the broad domestic and international policies that affect the nation's finances. Because the Treasury Department is the second-oldest executive department, the secretary is the second-ranking member of the president's cabinet. As the federal government's chief financial officer, the secretary of the Treasury is regularly called upon by Congress to provide detailed reports on the state of the nation's finances. In addition, the secretary serves on numerous committees and advisory groups involved with the management of federal funds and international monetary matters. The secretary is the U.S. governor of the International Monetary Fund (a specialized agency of the United Nations established to promote international monetary cooperation) and sits on the boards of a variety of other international banking organizations.

Assisting the secretary in the discharge of his duties is the deputy secretary, a position created in 1972. Also appointed by the president, the deputy secretary assists in the supervision and direction of the department and acts for the secretary in his absence.

Serving beneath the secretary and deputy secretary is a cadre of under secretaries, assistant secretaries, and deputy assistant secretaries, each of whom holds administrative responsibility for specific Treasury programs. The under secretary for finance advises the secretary on all domestic finance, banking, and economic matters, including the management of the public debt. The under secretary is aided by assistant secretaries for domestic finance and economic policy; a fiscal assistant secretary supervises the Treasury's financing operations and manages the cash balances. The under secretary for finance also oversees the work of the treasurer of the United States, who reviews

Secretary of the Treasury Nicholas F. Brady (left), President George Bush (center), and Attorney General Dick Thornburgh in a meeting at the White House in 1989. The secretary of the Treasury is the president's chief financial adviser and recommends domestic and international policies to promote the nation's economic growth.

currency production and redemption, signs all currency, and promotes the sale of savings bonds.

Additional assistant secretaries are concerned with the department's international affairs, enforcement operations, legislative affairs, management of the annual planning and budget processes, execution of domestic and international tax policies, and public affairs. Other top officials in the department include the general counsel, who furnishes legal advice, and the inspector general, who ensures that the department's programs are run efficiently and are free of corruption.

Although the upper-level officers, working out of the main Treasury building in Washington, D.C., advise and assist the secretary in the formation of overall policy, it is the Treasury Department's 11 bureaus, located throughout the nation, that put those policies into action. These offices carry out the bulk of the department's day-to-day operations, including its financial, law enforcement, taxation, coin and currency manufacture, and other vital functions.

The Bureau of Alcohol, Tobacco and Firearms

In 1972, the various sections of the Treasury Department involved in regulating the production, use, and distribution of alcohol and tobacco products and with the control of firearms and explosives were consolidated into the Bureau of Alcohol, Tobacco and Firearms. Of these former offices, the largest was the Alcohol Tax Unit (ATU), established within the Bureau of Internal Revenue following the repeal of Prohibition in 1933 to enforce the internal revenue laws affecting distilled spirits, wine, beer, and industrial alcohol.

One of the by-products of Prohibition during the 1920s and early 1930s was a rise in organized crime, as criminals were lured by the tremendous profits to be made in the illegal liquor trade. Along with the rise of organized crime came a proliferation of deadly weapons on the streets of the nation, in particular

Crime kingpin Al Capone, also known as Scarface (left), is transported to a federal penitentiary in 1932. During Prohibition, criminals such as Capone made fortunes in the illegal liquor trade. After the repeal of Prohibition in 1933, the Alcohol Tax Unit, predecessor of the Bureau of Alcohol, Tobacco and Firearms, investigated violations of the liquor laws.

machine guns and sawed-off shotguns. Alarmed by the rising use of firearms in crimes committed across the country, Congress responded with the passage of the National Firearms Act of 1934 and the Federal Firearms Act of 1938, two pieces of legislation designed to control the spread and use of deadly weapons by prohibiting sales of guns to convicted criminals and controlling interstate traffic in firearms. Ultimately, the responsibility for investigating violations of the firearms acts would fall upon ATU agents.

In 1951, the collection of taxes on tobacco products was added to ATU's growing roster of duties. With the increase in responsibilities came a name change, to the Alcohol and Tobacco Tax Division. Further gun control legislation in 1968 and added enforcement responsibilities prompted yet another change of title to the Alcohol, Tobacco and Firearms Division (ATF). In 1970, ATF was charged with regulating the explosives industry and curtailing the illegal possession of explosives. With its functions thus significantly enlarged, ATF was removed from the Internal Revenue Service, where it had resided for 40 years, and given separate bureau status.

Today, one of the most important functions of the Bureau of Alcohol, Tobacco and Firearms (also known by the acronym ATF) is controlling the misuse of firearms and keeping them out of the hands of criminals. Each year, ATF issues thousands of firearm licenses and permits to users, dealers, and manufacturers. And every year, in cooperation with state and local police, ATF agents confiscate thousands of illegal firearms and make thousands of arrests for federal gun law violations. Many of the crimes involving guns are solved with the help of ATF's National Firearms Tracing Center. Working with a nationwide network of manufacturers, importers, wholesalers, and dealers, and employing ATF's own extensive research facilities containing nearly 3,000 different models of firearms, the center can efficiently and effectively trace guns used in the commission of serious crimes. Each year ATF makes nearly 50,000 successful traces that lead to the solution of crimes.

Another important law enforcement function of ATF is the investigation of bombing incidents, a responsibility it shares with the Federal Bureau of Investigation and, in certain cases, with the Postal Inspection Service. ATF is in charge of investigations when illegal explosives are transported between states for the purpose of injuring people or destroying property, when a bombing is aimed against commercial properties, or when explosives damage Treasury Department buildings or operations. Two such incidents in the 1970s demonstrate the effectiveness of ATF explosives investigations. In Toledo, Ohio, nearly half a ton of deadly explosives was reported missing from a work site in 1975. ATF agents were immediately called to the scene and, working in

A special agent displays illegal firearms seized by the Bureau of Alcohol, Tobacco and Firearms (ATF) in Tampa, Florida. Each year the ATF confiscates thousands of illegal firearms; it also issues firearms licenses and permits to dealers, manufacturers, and users.

tandem with local law enforcement officers, quickly tracked down and arrested three individuals, recovering most of the explosives before they could be used or sold. In Greenville, South Carolina, ATF agents were called on to investigate the bombing of a textile mill in 1976. In the rubble of the explosion the agents discovered two sticks of dynamite still intact; the agents traced the explosives back to a local construction firm, which, surprisingly, had not realized the dynamite had been stolen. After further investigation, ATF agents identified and located the construction firm employee responsible for the theft. He, in turn, provided information that led to the arrest and conviction of the two men who had plotted and carried out the bombing. One of the men was the mill's owner. In addition to its investigatory work, ATF ensures that those involved in the legal explosives trade store their materials in a safe and secure manner, to avoid presenting a hazard to the public.

Although traffic in illicit distilled spirits has declined considerably since the days of Prohibition, ATF agents continue to locate, seize, and destroy illegal distilleries throughout the nation, along with thousands of gallons of "moonshine," as the illegal liquor is called. But most of the bureau's alcohol-related activities today involve the regulation of the revenue laws affecting hundreds of distilleries, wineries, and breweries operating legally in the United States. ATF has the responsibility of determining and ensuring the full collection of the taxes due from legal alcohol industries. Similarly, the bureau regulates and collects revenue from hundreds of tobacco producers and warehousers across America. Together, the tobacco and alcohol revenues collected by ATF each year amount to billions of dollars, forming the second largest source of federal revenue, behind the combined total of individual income and corporate income taxes.

The Office of the Comptroller
of the Currency

Since the creation of the Federal Reserve System in 1913, the comptroller of the currency's direct involvement with the actual distribution of U.S. currency has diminished greatly. Today, the office's relationship to currency is an indirect one, arising principally from the comptroller's administration of the country's national banks. Foremost, the Office of the Comptroller is responsible for ensuring that each federally chartered bank is soundly operated and that each member institution of the national banking system meets the public's need for commercial banking and trust services such as those provided by savings institutions. The comptroller accomplishes this primarily through the control of the federal bank charter process. All applications for a federal bank charter are first submitted to the Office of the Comptroller, which, after a detailed and lengthy examination of the bank's resources, management, and administration, either approves or rejects the application. Additionally, the comptroller grants permits for the formation of new branches of existing banks and for the merger of banks within the national system.

The Office of the Comptroller shares certain segments of its national bank supervision with the Federal Reserve Board, which supervises those state banks that are members of the Federal Reserve System. A third agency, the Federal Deposit Insurance Corporation, created in 1933 to ensure that depositors would not lose all their money in the event of a bank closure, regulates all federally insured banks that are not members of the Federal Reserve System.

The central concern of the comptroller of the currency remains the nearly 5,000 federally chartered national banks operating in the United States. The comptroller must see to it that the federal laws regulating the banks' operation are properly adhered to and carried out. Assisting the comptroller are 6 district deputy comptrollers and 6 district administrators who supervise a staff of nearly 1,800 bank examiners nationwide. These examiners periodically visit every national bank, closely inspect its operations, and report the results of their examinations to the comptroller. Their reports help the comptroller appraise the financial condition of the banks, the soundness of their operations, the quality of their management, and the extent of their compliance with the laws and regulations governing the nation's banking system.

Unlike most other federal agencies, the Office of the Comptroller of the Currency receives no appropriated funds for its operations. Instead, all of its expenses are met by fees and assessments levied against the banks it regulates.

The U.S. Customs Service

The U.S. Customs Service is responsible for certifying all persons and goods entering or leaving the United States and for assessing and collecting duties on imported merchandise. The tremendous growth in international trade and travel since World War II has made these tasks increasingly complex. In the 1950s, nearly 130 million people crossed the borders of the United States each year; by the 1980s, that number had more than doubled, with more than 260 million people—more than the population of the entire United States—traveling in and out of the country annually. Each year, millions of imported products stream through American ports, border stations, and international airports, and each shipment requires close inspection, assessment, and regulation by a customs officer.

Today, the Customs Service's mission to control the movement of people and products across the nation's borders has been made more difficult to accomplish because of the alarming increase in drug smuggling. Blocking the importation of narcotic and dangerous drugs into the country has been the responsibility of the Customs Service since Congress passed the first Narcotics Prohibition Act in 1909. When the problem reached epidemic proportions in the 1960s, the Customs Service devoted a greater part of its resources to battling the war on drugs. Although a portion of the responsibility for stemming the tide of illegal drugs was transferred to the Justice Department's newly created Drug Enforcement Administration in 1973, the Customs Service remained the main line of defense.

A U.S. Customs agent stops a driver as she crosses the Mexico-Texas border. The Customs Service checks all persons and goods entering or leaving the United States and collects duties on imported merchandise.

Employing a sophisticated network of high-speed boats, aircraft, helicopters, infrared sensors, radar, and communications equipment, customs agents annually seize illegal drugs worth millions of dollars. One of the most heralded cases in the Customs Service's long war on drugs began in 1970 at Miami International Airport in Florida. Acting on a tip that a major shipment of heroin would be entering the country from France by way of South America, customs agents began an intensive search of all suspect aircraft entering the country from the south. That search led to the discovery of 93 pounds of heroin concealed in the false bottoms of suitcases inside a small plane parked in Miami. Further investigation eventually resulted in the capture of an elusive and infamous smuggling ring headed by drug kingpin Auguste Riccord. Riccord and his cohorts in France and Latin America were charged with conspiring to smuggle into the United States more than 1,100 pounds of heroin, valued at

$250 million. The case would later become the inspiration for the movie *The French Connection*.

In their battle against drug smuggling Customs agents use dogs specially trained to sniff out drugs. First used on a wide scale in 1970, detector dogs enable agents to search vehicles, mail, baggage, and cargo ships in record time. In 30 minutes a dog and handler can check more than 500 packages; it would take a Customs mail examiner several days to inspect as many. In their first year on the job, detector dogs located more than $3 million worth of illegal drugs.

Although the apprehension of drug smugglers and the seizure of illegal drugs are perhaps the most publicized of the Customs Service's missions, they are by no means its sole enforcement activities. Customs agents are also charged with detecting and apprehending individuals engaged in such fraudulent commercial activities as patent, copyright, and trademark infringements. They confiscate materials that do not bear the mark of the country of origin as required by law, and they are on constant lookout for travelers illegally transporting liquor, guns, gold, jewelry, and pornography. As the government's principal border agency, the Customs Service is called upon to enforce more than 400 provisions on behalf of more than 40 other federal agencies, protecting endangered species, quarantining plants and animals hazardous to American agriculture, and ensuring the safety of imported vehicles and equipment. All of these responsibilities are carried out in addition to the Customs Service's principal task of assessing and collecting customs duties on goods imported into the United States; these duties annually add billions of dollars to the Treasury.

The Bureau of Engraving and Printing

Each year more than 40 billion documents, from paper currency and notes to postage stamps, come off the presses of the Treasury's Bureau of Engraving and Printing, making it the world's largest printer of security documents—stamps, notes, bonds, etc. Although the bureau prints materials for 75 different government departments and agencies, its principal product is paper currency. Today, nearly 99 percent of the currency produced by the bureau consists of the Federal Reserve notes in daily use, ranging in denomination from $1 to $100. Prior to 1969 the bureau also printed $500, $1,000, $5,000 and $10,000 notes; these larger denominations have since been discontinued.

The process of printing the nation's paper money involves a number of steps. When the design of a currency note has been approved by the secretary

A $10,000 Federal Reserve note. The Bureau of Engraving and Printing has not produced this denomination since 1969; however, Federal Reserve notes ranging in denomination from $1 to $100 are still printed.

of the Treasury—after the secretary has conferred with the director of the bureau, the treasurer of the United States, and the Federal Reserve Board—the design is given to the bureau's skilled engravers. Using delicate instruments, and working with the aid of magnifying glasses, the engravers cut the design into steel dies that will be used to form the master printing plate. The master plates are then loaded onto high-speed presses that turn out large printed sheets of uncut bills. These sheets are called "subjects" and contain 32 notes each. First the backs of the notes are printed with a specially produced green ink; after drying, the faces are printed in black ink the following day. Over 8,000 sheets an hour fly across the presses.

After the printers have printed the subject sheets, they examine the sheets for defects before cutting them in half—into sheets of 16 notes each. These sheets are run through the presses a second time to overprint the fronts with the Treasury seal and serial numbers in green ink and the Federal Reserve district seal in black ink. (The seal bears the name of one of the 12 district banks, such as "Federal Reserve Bank of St. Louis, Missouri" along with a letter: in this case the letter *H*, eighth in the alphabet, corresponding to the Federal Reserve's eighth district, of which St. Louis is the center.) Examiners once again check the notes before the sheets are sent to the huge paper cutters used to cut the sheets into individual notes. The finished notes are then packaged for shipment to Federal Reserve banks, where they enter circulation, primarily as replacements for worn or mutilated currency.

In addition to currency, the presses of the bureau print nearly 30 billion U.S.

A printer removes a large sheet of uncut bills from the master plate at the Bureau of Engraving and Printing. More than 8,000 sheets an hour fly off the Treasury's presses.

postage stamps each year. Although the design of new postage stamps rests with the U.S. Postal Service, the artists of the Bureau of Engraving and Printing actually repare the plates used in printing the stamps. As with currency, bureau examiners carefully inspect postage stamps for printing defects before they ship them to the Postal Service for distribution.

In all, the bureau is responsible for the printing and processing of more than 800 different products, including such diverse items as U.S. bonds, revenue stamps, food coupons, and White House invitations. The bureau also serves as an adviser to other federal agencies regarding the design and production of government documents that because of their value require special features to deter counterfeiting.

Because of the sensitive nature of its own printed products, the bureau maintains strict accounting procedures during the manufacturing process. Nevertheless, thefts have occurred from time to time. One of the bureau's biggest losses came in 1954, when workers discovered that two packages containing $160,000 in $20 notes were missing from the storage vault. The original packages had been replaced by two dummy parcels wrapped to resemble the genuine packages. Secret Service agents, responsible for the protection of the nation's currency, were called in to investigate. Working from a report by the Virginia State Police that some of the missing notes were circulating in their state, the agents followed a paper trail that eventually led to a bureau employee, formerly assigned to the currency wrapping section, who was arrested and later convicted of the theft.

The Federal Law Enforcement Training Center

In 1970, the Treasury established the Federal Law Enforcement Training Center in Glynco, Georgia, to help not only its own agents but those from other departments carry out their varied enforcement duties. Today, the center's programs provide training in special techniques and tactics for enforcement officers from 60 different federal agencies, including the U.S. Coast Guard. Both uniformed officers and special agents of the Treasury Department attend

A Treasury agent learns how to use a firearm at the Federal Law Enforcement Training Center in Glynco, Georgia. Officers at the Center also attend classes on such topics as the use of microcomputers as an investigative tool and how to detect counterfeit currency.

classes dealing with such issues of common concern as white-collar crime, the use of microcomputers as an investigative tool, and contract and procurement fraud (how to detect cheating in the purchase of government equipment, for example). Each course is designed to prepare Treasury agents for actual performance in the field and, ultimately, to enhance the quality and professionalism of each of the bureau's law enforcement officers.

The Financial Management Service

The original act creating the Treasury Department established a system under which the public money would be received, maintained, and disbursed. Originally, these accounting duties were performed by the register of the Treasury, with the custody of public funds vested in the treasurer of the United States. Over the years, however, as managing the nation's finances became a more complex process, these functions were gradually centralized in the Financial Management Service. Today, all responsibilities for maintaining the government's central accounting and reporting system reside in the service, upon which the president, Congress, and the public rely for information about the state of the public finances. Toward that end, the service periodically publishes reports on the government's financial operations. The reports describe, among other things, the federal government's cash assets (everything that it owns and what is owed to it) and related liabilities (payments due to suppliers, salaries due to employees, and other debts that it owes), the status of appropriations approved by Congress, and receipts and expenditures showing surpluses or deficits. In addition, the service reports contain detailed statements of all deposits and withdrawals made in the government's accounts maintained in Federal Reserve banks and branches and of the amount of U.S. currency and coin in circulation.

One of the most important functions of the Financial Management Service is to disburse more than 500 million Treasury checks—and perform nearly 250 million electronic fund transfers (which transmit money electronically from one account to another by using computers)—each year. The money is used for payment of all federal salaries and wages, for all payments to suppliers of goods and services to the government, and for all payments made under such federal benefits programs as Social Security and veterans' pensions. The service also pays all Treasury checks and reconciles the cash outflow against the accounts of the various federal government disbursing officers. In addition, the service examines all claims of forged government checks and checks that are lost, stolen, or destroyed, and it issues new checks for approved claims.

By working closely with other agencies and by issuing guidelines and regulations to assist them in instituting proper methods of paying, collecting, and receiving federal funds, the service seeks to improve financial management practices throughout the government.

The Internal Revenue Service

The increased economic activity of the 1950s, with its burgeoning employment and production, raised income tax collections to unprecedented levels. To handle the increased revenues, the Internal Revenue Service (IRS) was substantially reorganized, and the administration of the tax laws decentralized from its Washington, D.C., headquarters to offices located throughout the country. Today, 7 regional commissioners of internal revenue and 62 district offices (at least one located in every state of the union) carry out the business of the IRS.

In 1961, the IRS significantly expanded its operations when it replaced its manual system of processing tax forms with a high-speed, automatic data processing system. Modified over the years, the system is currently capable of handling the more than 100 million tax returns and the half billion related documents now filed by taxpayers. Using the IRS data processing system, 10 regional service centers receive and process the income tax forms mailed by taxpayers across the nation. As the tax returns are processed, the information contained on the forms is transferred to magnetic tape, which is then electronically fed to the National Computer Center in Martinsburg, West Virginia. There the data is retained on a master file and stored along with the records of each individual taxpayer's account. The National Computer Center then forwards the list of all taxpayers who are due refunds or owe money to the Financial Management Service.

Despite the increased efficiency of electronic processing, the initial step of completing the income tax form can still be a puzzling process for the average taxpayer. To help citizens find their way through the complex filing procedures, the IRS established a taxpayer service organization, offering telephone assistance and various public information programs. It also created the problem resolution program, designed to solve taxpayers' complaints that, for whatever reason, are not relieved through normal channels.

Computer tapes at the National Computer Center in Martinsburg, West Virginia. The Internal Revenue Service's master file containing all taxpayers' accounts is kept at the National Computer Center.

In addition to the income tax, the IRS assesses and collects taxes on corporate incomes, on estates (heirs to valuable property must pay taxes on that property), and on gifts (people who give large sums of money to others must fill out a gift tax return and pay the tax due). It also regulates the administration of various excise taxes. But it is income taxes, along with social security taxes, that are the major focus of the service's staff and programs. Each year the IRS collects more than $400 billion from American taxpayers, making the income tax the largest single source of income for the federal government.

The U.S. Mint

Since the founding of the U.S. Mint in 1792, its principal function has been producing the millions of coins used daily by Americans. In the intervening years, there have been a number of changes in the types, denominations, and contents of coins produced for circulation. Half-cent, two-cent, three-cent, and twenty-cent pieces, all originally authorized by Congress and formerly produced by the mint, have long since been discontinued. The silver half-dime was replaced by the now familiar nickel in 1866. And gold coins were withdrawn from circulation in 1933. Gradually these coins were replaced by those now commonly found in circulation: the Lincoln penny, introduced in 1909 on the 100th anniversary of Abraham Lincoln's birth; the Jefferson nickel, first minted in 1938 on the 200th anniversary of Thomas Jefferson's birth; the Roosevelt dime, issued following the death of President Franklin D. Roosevelt in 1945; and the Washington quarter, first circulated in 1932 on the 200th anniversary of George Washington's birth. The Kennedy half-dollar, first issued in 1964 following the assassination of President John F. Kennedy, and the Eisenhower dollar, released in 1971 in honor of the late president Dwight D. Eisenhower, are also minted in smaller amounts and released for circulation.

By law, U.S. coin designs change infrequently; once a design has been approved and is in production, it cannot be changed for 25 years except by a special act of Congress. Nevertheless, new coin designs do occasionally appear. In tribute to the nation's bicentennial in 1976, the designs on the reverse, or back, of the quarter, half-dollar, and dollar were temporarily changed to patriotic scenes associated with the nation's founding. The reverse of the quarter depicted a colonial drummer; that of the half-dollar featured Independence Hall in Philadelphia, where the Declaration of Independence was signed in 1776; and the dollar showed the Liberty Bell and the moon. The obverse, or front, of the coins remained the same, with the exception of the

105

dates "1776–1976," which appeared at the bottom of each coin. At the end of the bicentennial year, the special designs went out of production. More recently, in 1979, Congress approved an entirely new type of dollar coin, much smaller in size and weight than the traditional dollar, and featuring the likeness of Susan B. Anthony, the noted women's rights advocate. The new coin met with much public dissatisfaction, however, perhaps because of its close resemblance to the quarter, and it was soon removed from production.

Today, mints operating in Philadelphia, Pennsylvania, and Denver, Colorado, produce the majority of the nation's coins. In addition, the San Francisco Assay Office in California issues a small number of coins. Silver is no longer used in the production of any coins currently in circulation; beginning in 1965, all quarters and dimes became "clad," that is, composed of an outer layer of copper and nickel bonded to an inner core of pure copper. In 1971, both the half-dollar and dollar also became clad coins. Today's nickel contains 75 percent copper and 25 percent nickel; the penny is 95 percent copper and 5 percent zinc.

To produce the metal used in the clad coins, the copper and nickel outer layer is created by melting the two metals together; the resulting metal alloy is then cast into ingots (bricklike blocks), and the ingots are rolled out into thin strips. A soft copper sheet is then sandwiched between the alloy strips to make a clad strip, and the whole is once again rolled out to the desired thickness of the coin. The clad strip is run through a blanking press, which punches out the rough coins. The blanks, traveling across a vibrating mesh, are separated from the unused metal and are then annealed (heated to soften them) and cleaned. When ready, the blanks are run through a coining press, where the actual design is stamped, using dies prepared by craftsmen at the U.S. Mint. Each coin is then inspected, weighed, counted, bagged, and sent to a storage vault before being sent out to the Federal Reserve Banks for circulation.

Along with coins issued for regular circulation, the U.S. Mint makes available to collectors special proof sets of coins currently in circulation, made from carefully selected blanks that have been given a high polish. The mint also manufactures commemorative coins, military medals, and, by contract, a small amount of coins for foreign governments.

In addition to its coining operations, the U.S. Mint is responsible for the production and safekeeping of the gold and silver bars that form the nation's reserves. Most of the monetary gold and silver stocks of the United States are stored in two high-security depositories, each under the supervision of U.S. Mint officials; silver is held at the U.S. Bullion Depository in West Point, New York, and gold is kept at the Fort Knox Bullion Depository in Kentucky.

The Bureau of the Public Debt

When Congress authorizes the federal government to borrow money, through the issuance of bonds or other securities, the Bureau of the Public Debt handles the transaction on behalf of the Treasury Department. From its headquarters in Washington, D.C., the bureau prepares the informational circulars that provide investors with details and instructions relating to each offering of public debt securities. It also administers all aspects of the sale. These securities include Treasury bills, which are short-term investments in minimum denominations of $10,000, purchased at a discount of their face value and maturing in either 3, 6, or 12 months; Treasury notes, which are medium-term investments with maturities from 1 to 10 years; and Treasury bonds, which are long-term investments that must be held from 10 to 30 years before the investor can redeem them at full value.

The bureau orders, stores, and distributes all public debt securities offered by the Treasury and maintains the accounts of the owners of these registered securities. When interest accrues on the securities, it is the bureau that authorizes the issuance of the payment checks. When, for any reason, a public debt security is lost, stolen, destroyed, or mutilated, bureau experts are sent to investigate the claim and to determine whether or not it is just and whether or not the security should be replaced.

Under the supervision of the bureau, transactions in public debt securities are held at various Federal Reserve Banks and their branches, acting in their role as fiscal agents of the United States.

The U.S. Savings Bonds Division

The Treasury Department's defense bond drives of World War II proved so effective that, at the war's end, the program was continued under a peacetime Savings Bonds Division. Today, the program remains one of the government's most popular public securities offerings. The division, through field offices located across the nation, promotes the purchase of two types of savings bonds: the Series EE Bond, an appreciation-type security that increases in redemption value, sold at 50 percent of the face value; and the Series HH Bond, a current-income security sold at face value on which a specified amount of interest is paid by Treasury check every six months. Like other registered securities offered by the federal government, savings bonds are essentially indestructible; that is, if lost, stolen, or destroyed, they will be replaced.

The Series EE Bond, issued by the U.S. Savings Bonds Division, is sold at 50 percent of the face value and is redeemable at face value upon full maturity. If lost, stolen, or destroyed, these bonds will be replaced by the federal government.

Through the Payroll Savings Plan, offered by employers, the Bond-A-Month plan, available at various financial institutions that act as issuing agents for the division, and with the help of a dedicated nationwide corps of volunteers who regularly hold bond drives, the division makes savings bonds widely available.

The U.S. Secret Service

The U.S. Secret Service is perhaps best known today for its role as the president's bodyguard. But protecting the integrity of the nation's money continues to be an important responsibility of the Secret Service. In its pursuit of counterfeiters the Secret Service has been particularly effective; most Americans today readily accept and pay out money without stopping to think that it may in fact be fake. Advances in photography, photocopying, and printing, all technologies readily accessible to would-be criminals, have raised the quality of counterfeit money to new heights, requiring closer examination to detect fraudulent currency and increasing the enforcement problems of the Secret Service. Consequently, to suppress counterfeiting activities, the Secret Service relies not only on intensive investigation and improved enforcement techniques but also on the education of the general public. Through informational notices and the posting of circulars at banks, stores, and other places where money regularly changes hands, the Secret Service informs the average person how to detect counterfeit money and what to do about it. It thus enlists the aid of every American in battling counterfeiters.

One of the Secret Service's most spectacular counterfeiting cases occurred in 1963, when agents apprehended nine men operating a sophisticated counterfeit ring out of San Francisco, California. When agents arrested the members of the ring, they found in their possession more than $2 million in counterfeit $20 and $50 bills; it was the single largest amount of counterfeit money seized up to that time.

In addition to detecting and arresting counterfeiters of currency, coins, and stamps, the Secret Service is regularly called upon to investigate cases dealing with the forgery of government checks and bonds. Thousands of government checks fail to reach their intended destinations because they are stolen and cashed by thieves posing as the rightful owners. And each year special agents of the Secret Service track down and arrest individuals involved in the forging of these checks.

In 1984, Congress passed legislation that expanded the Secret Service's duties to include investigating credit card and computer fraud. Agents combat the counterfeiting of commercial credit cards and investigate fraud related to the electronic funds transfer system (EFTS) of the Treasury Department. In

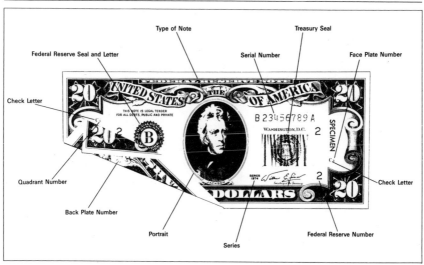

Positions of the important features on a genuine $20 bill. The U.S. Secret Service was created in 1865 to combat counterfeiting. Today, the Secret Service continues to train its agents to recognize the differences between genuine and counterfeit money.

Secret Service agents surround president-elect George Bush's limousine as it makes its way through the inaugural parade on January 20, 1989. The Secret Service's most visible job is to protect the president, members of his family, the vice-president, and other high-ranking officials.

this system, money is transmitted electronically from one account to another by computer. Transfers made by the Treasury to regional banks and other financial institutions must be protected against possible illegal practices. The Secret Service closely monitors the computers, analyzes printouts, and searches for irregularities. If something appears improper, agents launch an investigation.

But the Secret Service's most visible function remains its protection of the president of the United States, members of his family, the vice-president, and other high-ranking officials. The discharge of that duty has never been easy, as the assassination of President John F. Kennedy in 1963 tragically illustrated. As a result of the assassination, Congress in 1965 extended Secret Service protection to include former presidents and their wives; subsequent legislation provided protection for the widows of former presidents until their remarriage or death, minor children of former presidents until they are 16 years old, and major presidential and vice-presidential candidates.

Additional protection for the president and his family is provided by the

Uniformed Division, a security unit that operates under the supervision of the Secret Service. Established in 1970, the Uniformed Division is charged with protecting the White House grounds, guarding buildings in which presidential offices are located, and acting as security officers at foreign diplomatic missions located in and around the nation's capital. A second uniformed security unit under the direction of the Secret Service is the Treasury Security Force, responsible for protecting the main Treasury building and the Treasury annex in Washington, D.C., and standing guard over the millions of dollars in securities and currency stored within the buildings.

From time to time, other protective duties are assigned to the Secret Service on a temporary basis. In December 1941, with the bombing of Pearl Harbor and the fear of an attack on mainland America, the Secret Service was called upon to protect and secure the nation's most treasured historic documents, including the original copies of the Declaration of Independence, the Constitution of the United States, and Lincoln's Second Inaugural Address. Under Secret Service guard, the documents were secretly removed from the Library of Congress in Washington, D.C., and transported to a hiding place. At the war's end, the documents were safely returned to Washington under the protection of the Secret Service.

Secretary of the Treasury Nicholas F. Brady in 1989. Brady pledged to work with President Bush and Congress to eliminate the nation's staggering budget deficit.

SIX

The Future of the Treasury Department

The challenges confronting the Treasury Department today may seem drastically different from those encountered two centuries ago. The United States is a more expansive, more populated, and more complicated nation operating in a more dangerous world. The national debt, once measured in millions of dollars, now reaches into the trillions and shows little sign of being easily diminished. Balancing the rising cost of running the federal government, the need for greater revenues, and the public's sometimes outright hostility to taxation makes for a frustrating and complex situation.

But the basic challenges facing the Treasury Department remain the same: to formulate and recommend to Congress and the president sound economic, financial, tax, and fiscal policies; to administer the tax laws firmly but evenhandedly; to act as the U.S. government's fiscal agent; to diligently enforce the laws; and to provide the coins and currency vital to the daily transactions of each American.

The technology available to meet those challenges, however, has changed dramatically. Today the Treasury Department is seeking to fit the advances of the modern age to existing programs and use them to carry the department effectively into the future.

As the ever-growing volume of income tax returns and documents pushes

113

the people and machines of the Internal Revenue Service to the limit, the IRS, out of necessity, must search for practical alternatives that will help solve its problems. Today, the IRS is in the midst of testing a new system that will bypass the costly method of processing paper tax returns. Called "electronic filing," the system is designed to accept returns from the computers of qualified tax preparation firms directly into the IRS system. With the number of tax returns already prepared by privately operated computers estimated to be about 13 million and growing rapidly, electronic filing holds the promise not only of faster, more accurate service to the taxpayer, but of savings to the government.

Similarly, the United States Customs Service is working hard to fully automate its collection of revenues, to help speed and track the movement of freight through ports, to reduce the paperwork needed for each shipment of imports, and to collect the duties in a more accurate and more secure manner. The Financial Management Service has increased its efficiency through the development of the Treasury Financial Communication System (TFCS), a computer-to-computer link with the Federal Reserve System that allows for the electronic transfer of funds to virtually any financial institution in the United States.

Such modern technologies, however, also pose new enforcement challenges for the Treasury Department. The Secret Service, for example, once faced primarily with counterfeiters turning out fraudulent currency with homemade plates and printing presses, now finds itself increasingly concerned with detecting and arresting offenders involved in computer access fraud, the illegal transfer of funds electronically. In order to stay one step ahead of the growing sophistication of criminals, Treasury enforcement officers are continually devising new methods and tactics to suppress crime. Scientists at the Bureau of Alcohol, Tobacco and Firearms laboratories have developed advanced analytical techniques used in explosives investigations. The computer-based Treasury Enforcement Communications System (TECS) allows agents to check instantly on suspicious individuals, vessels, aircraft, and vehicles. Research conducted by the Customs Service has proven the applicability of nuclear magnetic resonance imaging technology in quickly detecting cocaine, heroin, and morphine in letter mail. (A letter is surrounded by an electromagnetic field and the amount of energy absorbed is then analyzed. This information is used to create a computerized, two-dimensional image that detects the presence of narcotics.)

But perhaps the greatest challenge facing the department today is neither office efficiency nor law enforcement; it is the challenge of the nation's staggering debt. The problem is not new; every generation of Treasury officers since the nation's founding has had to wrestle with the problem of federal debt. Although the Department of the Treasury has been vested with the responsibility for managing the public debt, it is not the Treasury that creates the debt. That responsibility rests with the president and Congress. It is only by adopting and adhering to fiscally sound policies and proposing and approving deficit-free balanced budgets that the president and Congress can begin to lead the nation down the long road toward reducing the national debt.

Department of the Treasury

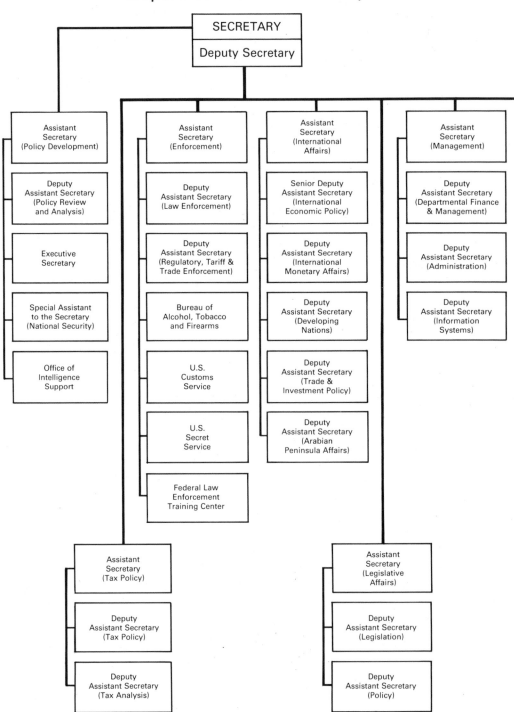

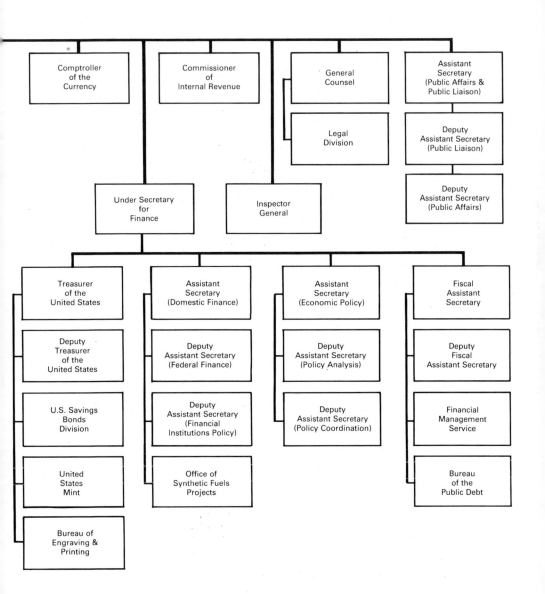

| Comptroller of the Currency | Commissioner of Internal Revenue | General Counsel | Assistant Secretary (Public Affairs & Public Liaison) |

Legal Division

Deputy Assistant Secretary (Public Liaison)

Deputy Assistant Secretary (Public Affairs)

Under Secretary for Finance

Inspector General

Treasurer of the United States

Assistant Secretary (Domestic Finance)

Assistant Secretary (Economic Policy)

Fiscal Assistant Secretary

Deputy Treasurer of the United States

Deputy Assistant Secretary (Federal Finance)

Deputy Assistant Secretary (Policy Analysis)

Deputy Fiscal Assistant Secretary

U.S. Savings Bonds Division

Deputy Assistant Secretary (Financial Institutions Policy)

Deputy Assistant Secretary (Policy Coordination)

Financial Management Service

United States Mint

Office of Synthetic Fuels Projects

Bureau of the Public Debt

Bureau of Engraving & Printing

GLOSSARY

Assessor   An official who determines the value of property for the purpose of taxation.

Bond   An interest-bearing certificate of public or private indebtedness. The borrower pays interest for the use of the money and must repay the amount of the bond by a specified date.

Bullion   Uncoined gold or silver in bar form.

Commodities   Economic goods such as products of agriculture or mining.

Comptroller   A public official who audits government accounts and sometimes certifies expenditures.

Counterfeit   To make an imitation of something with the intent to deceive.

Currency   A medium of exchange (coins, paper money, bank notes) valid for general public circulation.

Excise tax   A tax levied on the manufacture, transportation, sale, or consumption of goods within a country.

Fiscal   Of or pertaining to the treasury or finances of a nation or branch of government.

Greenback   A legal-tender note issued by the U.S. government.

New Deal   The legislative and administrative program of President Franklin D. Roosevelt designed to promote economic recovery and social reform during the 1930s.

Revenue   The yield of sources of income (such as taxes) that a nation or state collects and receives into its treasury for public use.

Stock share   Any of the equal parts into which the entire value of a company is divided. It represents ownership in the company.

Tariff   A schedule of taxes imposed by a government on imported, or in some countries exported, goods.

SELECTED REFERENCES

Browning, Peter. *The Treasury and Economic Policy, 1964–1985*. New York: Longman, 1986.

Chommie, John C. *The Internal Revenue Service*. New York: Praeger, 1970.

Gloss, John Dean. *A History of Tariff Administration in the U.S.* New York: AMS Press, 1968.

Kimmel, Louis Henry. *Federal Budget and Fiscal Policy, 1789–1958*. Washington, DC: Brookings Institution, 1959.

Matusky, Gregory, and John P. Hayes. *The U.S. Secret Service*. New York: Chelsea House, 1988.

Nussbaum, Arthur. *History of the Dollar*. New York: Columbia University Press, 1957.

Studensky, Paul, and Herman F. Krooss. *Financial History of the United States: Fiscal, Monetary, Banking, and Tariff*. New York: McGraw-Hill, 1963.

Taus, Esther Rogoff. *The Role of the U.S. Treasury in Stabilizing the Economy, 1941–1946*. Washington, DC: University Press of America, 1981.

Taylor, Gary. *The Federal Reserve System*. New York: Chelsea House, 1989.

Taylor, Jack. *The Internal Revenue Service*. New York: Chelsea House, 1987.

Turell, John Upton. *The U.S. Department of the Treasury*. New York: Duell, Sloan and Pearce, 1963.

U.S. Department of the Treasury. *Domestic and Foreign Coins Manufactured by Mints of the U.S., 1973–1980*. Washington, DC: Government Printing Office, 1981.

Watson, Jesse P. *Bureau of the Mint*. Baltimore: Johns Hopkins University Press, 1926.

Whitehead, Donald. *Border Guard, The Story of the U.S. Customs Service*. New York: McGraw-Hill, 1963.

Wolman, Paul. *The U.S. Mint*. New York: Chelsea House, 1987.

INDEX

121

Mark Walston served in the Department of the Treasury as a historian with the United States Customs Service. He holds a B.A. in U.S. history and an M.A. in American studies from the University of Maryland. He has published numerous articles in popular and professional journals, including *Maryland Historical Magazine, Victorian Institute Journal, Potomac Almanac,* and *Washingtonian.* He is currently a free-lance writer based in Olney, Maryland.

Arthur M. Schlesinger, jr., served in the White House as special assistant to Presidents Kennedy and Johnson. He is the author of numerous acclaimed works in American history and has twice been awarded the Pulitzer Prize. He taught history at Harvard College for many years and is currently Albert Schweitzer Professor of the Humanities at the City College of New York.